The Storm of a Lifetime

A Report to U.S. Catholic Bishops and Pope Francis

J, M & J

John Brian Driscoll

OLD GLORY BOOKS
HELENA, MONTANA
2016

The Storm of a Lifetime
Copyright © 2016 John B. Driscoll

ISBN: 0615855148
ISBN-13: 978-0615-85514-1

Cover Design: Seth Roby, Colorblind Prints, Helena, Montana
Art: O'Brien Driscoll, age 7, St. Mary's Peak and St. Mary's Mission

Other Non-Fiction by John B. Driscoll

"The Guns, They Hear Me"

DEDICATION

To Bishop Hunthausen and Pope Francis,
Faith and Justice

Western Montana Diocese Bishop Hunthausen celebrating Mass
on St. Mary's Peak, Feast of the Assumption, 1965
Photo by John Bryan Driscoll, Jr.

CONTENTS

AUTHOR'S NOTE

One hundred seventy-five years ago a Belgian priest named Father Pierre DeSmet, S.J. established and helped build the St. Mary's Mission church portrayed on this report's cover. As he responded to the spiritual needs of Indians, he witnessed the viciousness of European-Americans toward them. In 1868, he wrote to a friend:

> I have been assured on good authority, that reckless endeavors are made in the new western settlements to continue the war with the Indians. It brings them money in abundance and they are determined to have it.[1]

The same rationalizations and viciousness protect the behavior that underlies our current perpetual world war. The biblical word persecution, subjecting someone to targeted hostility and ill-treatment, especially because of race or political or religious beliefs, best describes the tactics and strategy of interests working to counter the nuclear age spiritual leadership of Archbishop Hunthausen. Persecution will be the price paid to reduce future numbers of nuclear weapons' detonations.

Continuing to reduce America's share of the world's nuclear arms requires commitment by all Catholics. Without a broad agreement that overcomes the purposeful cultivation of division with wedge-issues and the national influence of entities which profit from contracting, manufacturing and conducting elements of U.S. defense and nuclear policy, we are Phaetons. That mythical Greek god prevailed on his father, Helios, to be able to ride the Sun in a chariot around the sky for a single day. He failed to control his horses. They swooped too low, scorched the earth and ate him.

Appendices to this report present Archbishop Hunthausen's case for non-violent action against nuclear weapons and President Reagan's speech to the Knights and Dames of the Sovereign Order of Malta.[2] Two others allow comparison of Navy Secretary John Lehman's speech condemning unilateral

1

disarmament, with President Harry Truman's dedication of the Temple of the Four Chaplains who gave up their life preservers in order for others to live.[3] The last compares the lives of Melvyn Paisley and Archbishop Jean Jadot.

This story of happenings inside the Catholic Church shows a grave division between ardent carriers of Roman Catholic traditions out of Old Europe and Indigenous American Catholics, formed in part by Europe's Missionary Church. Seeds of healing also appear. When Ronald Reagan, the Great Communicator, gave his last speech as President of the United States at the Waldorf-Astoria Hotel in New York City, he opened the next door for us. He likened the Order of Malta to Thomas Jefferson's idea of a "natural aristocracy." This was an honor only a catholic, as distinct from "Catholic," Indigenous American could bestow. The seating diagram for that evening's head table included Francis Bessenyey. Years later, in good humor he intimated that the Order of Malta is all about titles and in the United States not many people have any. "They needed me at the head table for my titles."[4] He headed the Hungarian Order of Malta, organized in exile during Communist control of his home country. He was as much a natural aristocrat as is Dutch Hunthausen. With the door of mutual respect open to all of us, and swinging both ways, we Catholics guided by our consciences can heal division inside the Catholic Church and, with Christ-like examples set by pastoral prelates, eliminate nuclear weapons with non-violent action.

NOTES

[1] Reverend Pierre-Jean De Smet, S.J., *Life, Letters and Travels of Father DeSmet Among the North American Indians*, page 1222, archive.org

[2] Author did not interview Archbishop Hunthausen. To gain access to Federal Bureau of Investigation (FBI) and Naval Investigative Services (NIS) files about Hunthausen, since he is still living, author did secure his signature on the Freedom of Information/Privacy Act FOIPA request form by contacting Father

Michael Ryan, former Chancellor of the Archdiocese of Seattle, Washington.

[3] Author tried unsuccessfully, on three separate occasions, to secure telephone and face-to-face interviews with former Secretary of Navy John F. Lehman.

[4] Author interviewed Francis Bessenyey at Hamilton, Montana http://missoulian.com/news/local/obituaries/francis-bakach-bessenyey/article_6b9cee86-4c75-11e2-b051-0019bb2963f4.html

CATHEDRAL-SIZED SCALE OF A TRIDENT NUCLEAR SUBMARINE

4

1. DELUSIONS OF POWER

Beneath a sleeping volcano, inside Seattle and Tacoma's shared International Airport, a man dressed in black stepped from a jet-way into a concourse filled with lights, cameras, microphones and reporters. Archbishop James Hickey might have slipped unannounced into the Pacific Northwest on November 2, 1983, except that he had been forced to ask Seattle's Archbishop Raymond Hunthausen to release a joint statement downplaying his upcoming visit.[5] Hickey wanted to pre-empt misunderstanding caused by a mysterious leak emanating from the U.S. East Coast.[6] On October 27, the two archbishops made Seattle front-page news, pushing back reports of 400 Koreans protesting the September 1 Soviet shoot-down of Korea Airlines Flight 007 and funeral plans for Washington State Democrat U.S. Senator Henry "Scoop" Jackson.[7] Jackson was the man responsible for making the Puget Sound home to hundreds of Trident nuclear missiles. They are deployed through the Hood Canal in huge submarines or stored at their base, the naval ammunition supply point at Bangor, Washington. "The Senator from Boeing" also helped advance Boeing Corporation's nuclear capable B-52 bombers and Minuteman and Cruise missiles.[8] Unknown to anyone in the U.S., when Hickey arrived in Seattle, the Soviets perceived signs of a nuclear attack on their country by the U.S and its NATO allies.

Real world events caused the Soviets to conclude that our military exercises were hiding a surprise nuclear attack in peacetime. After unusually aggressive fleet exercises by the U.S and the Soviet downing of KAL 007 as a spy plane, NATO military activity increased. Eight weeks earlier 170 long-range aircraft, flying on radio silence, transported 16,044 U.S. troops with their personal equipment and arms to West Germany. Drawing pre-positioned armored and wheeled vehicles, they and many other troops closed on the border with East Germany and Czechoslovakia. The world's airwaves filled with an October burst of secret communications conforming to doctrinal templates for

"Nuclear consultation in NATO." Soviet intelligence failed to assess that encrypted U.S. and U.K traffic was a pre-cursor to the October 25 U.S. invasion of the Queen of England's tiny island of Granada. As Hickey arrived in Seattle, even more activity, personnel and communications had begun to emanate from NATO's operational war-fighting centers.

In Seattle, most were wondering if Hickey's Apostolic Visitation had arrived, because Hunthausen had been such an effective protestor against nuclear weapons.[9] Hickey foreclosed all the local conjecturing by immediately saying, "Hunthausen's controversial protests against nuclear weapons are not an issue."[10] According to the Washington D.C. prelate, he and his two assistants came to discuss "internal church matters."[11] This rhetorical distinction marked the public beginning of a "wounding and unjust process" for Hunthusen, originating everywhere and nowhere.[12] The investigators stayed long enough to record between 67 and 80 secret papal depositions from the clergy, religious, and laity and to review documents.[13] They engaged Hunthausen in nearly five hours of intense discussion.[14] Six days later they departed Seattle at the height of the worst nuclear war scare since the Cuban Missile Crisis. As Hickey stepped back into the jet-way for his trans-continental flight, the Soviets were expecting a surprise U.S. nuclear attack within 36 hours and had already begun their doctrinal response, which is to strike sooner with their own nuclear weapons.

On November 7, NATO forces began the five-day ABLE ARCHER command post exercise at DEFCON 5, simulating the Command, Control and Communication messaging through DEFCON 1, which, as learned later, KGB agents were reporting as real. Having studied U.S. nuclear war-fighting doctrine, the Soviets realized Operational Readiness No. 1, or DEFCON 1, is declared when there are obvious indications of preparations to begin military operations. U.S. Doctrine considers war as inevitable and may start at any moment. To simulate an actual nuclear release, British Prime Minister Margaret Thatcher and West German Chancellor Helmut Kohl began participating. At the last minute, Robert McFarlane, the new National Security Advisor to Reagan, canceled participation by President Reagan, Vice President George H.W. Bush, and Secretary of Defense Casper Weinberger. Based upon his own military experience, McFarlane appropriately sensed the escalatory messages being conveyed. The crisis ended on November 11 during the same hours Hickey sat in his Hyattsville chancery finalizing the report of his visitation.[15]

Ten days later, after opening an exhibition of Vatican Art in San Francisco, the Vatican Secretary of State Cardinal Agostino Casaroli arrived in Washington D.C.. Casaroli stayed in the Vatican's Apostolic Delegation on Massachusetts Avenue across from the Naval Observatory quarters of Vice President Bush. On November 22, Casaroli and Apostolic Delegate, Archbishop Pio Laghi, joined the family of President John F. Kennedy for a Mass marking JFK's assassination. Inside Georgetown University's Holy Trinity Church, Hickey delivered the homily to seated dignitaries, including Reagan.[16] He focused on the dangers of nuclear weapons.[17] That afternoon Casaroli and Laghi met informally with Reagan. [18] They met again at the White House November 23. This last meeting finalized details of U.S. formal recognition of the Holy See.[19] With formal recognition set to happen, Casaroli returned to the Vatican, causing and coinciding with whispered praises in the hallways speaking of Hunthausen as "a man of Vatican II."[20] One journalist in Rome reported, "Those in the papal apartment who have seen Hickey's report firmly believe it exemplifies the gulf between the Vatican and the Catholic Church in the United States."[21]Meanwhile at the White House, a single letter of support for formal recognition of the Holy See had arrived from an American citizen. The correspondent was a Catholic priest living in Oshkosh, Wisconsin.

Fifty-one year old Father Regis Barwig, a member of the Order of Malta since 1971, who had worked with Cardinal Cicognani, the Vatican's Secretary of State from 1961 to 1969, had typed his letter five days after attending the November 19 opening of the Vatican Museum Arts Exhibition in San Francisco.[22]

On that day in San Francisco, he said Mass with Casaroli, his old colleague under Cicognani, and had dinner with Reagan's Personal Envoy to the Vatican, William Wilson, Barwig's friend since 1971. According to Barwig, Casaroli informed his concelebrants that "clearance had effectively been granted by the legislature for establishment of diplomatic relations with the Holy See." Wilson talked with Barwig throughout the evening:

> Because Wilson and I were friends and because I was closely associated with Archbishop [later Cardinal] Cicognani in his latter years in Rome, I saw the overall usefulness of our recognition of the Holy See.[23]

Barwig wrote Reagan that the U.S. would be better able to discern the degree to which domestic Catholics and Catholic institutions reflect the "authentic" positions of the Holy See. He said:

> This will clarify the authority which Catholics, individually and corporately, speak to social and political issues, often ostensibly in behalf of the Church.

He expected that marginal and eccentric positions espoused by individual Catholics:

> . . . at times uncongenial if not inimical to those of the Holy See and/or the United States, could be more precisely described as purely private opinions and rendered less noxious.

Barwig was concerned about the imminent danger of the Catholic Church in the U.S. being linked to the policies of one political party. He told Reagan:

> There is a subtle and insidious movement in some quarters to link the Pro-Life/Right-to-Life Movement to the call for a nuclear freeze, unilateral disarmament, and pacifism.

He considered this effort to be pro-abortion and/or interested in downgrading the importance of national defense:

> There is here an effort to court and win Catholic support for positions which run counter to the Church's authentic

teaching by placing them under one pro-life umbrella, which would step-by-step become increasingly anti-life and anti-defense.

He concluded it would be disastrous for Catholics to fall prey indirectly to the manipulation of unscrupulous politicians, espousing shortsighted and harmful moral, and social and defense policies.[24] Ms. Kathy Osborne, Reagan's Personal Secretary, reviewed the letter and commented on a note to Richard Darman, Assistant to the President, "I'm not sure how Barwig got the 1669 [Postal] code, but I question whether RR needs to personally see."[25]

From Rome two weeks later, Cardinal Joseph Ratzinger, Prefect for the Doctrine of the Faith, wrote Hunthausen that he had received the report of the visitation.[26] Hickey's final report and personal papers, still unseen by Hunthausen, now lie in the Vatican's Secret Archives.[27] Hickey's assistant, Father William Coyle's notes are not in the Archives for the Redemptorist Province of Denver.[28] Those and other related notes may now be in the Archdiocese of Seattle's secret archives.[29] This practice is not to protect Hunthausen, who specifically requested that any investigation of him be conducted in the open.[30] Ratzinger employed secrecy, using the Vatican Secretary of State's regulation, *Secreta Continere,* which authorizes pontifical secrets based upon ten types of actions, including "Notifications sent to the Congregation for the Doctrine of the Faith about teachings and publications and the Congregation's examination of them" and "Reports by papal legates on matters required by pontifical secrecy."[31] Catholics leaking knowledge of the Apostolic Visitation risked excommunication.

In spite of potential penalty for those who might communicate openly about the secret process, I had already been personally made aware that something big, bad and secret was about to happen to Hunthausen two months before the Apostolic Visitation.[32] The information came to me from an American General in a pitch-dark German forest, while I was helping prepare tracked vehicles for rail movement to the Inner-German

Border.[33] At about that time, 1250 persons were gathering in Seattle's Saint James Cathedral for a Mass sponsored by Dignity, a homosexual support group.[34] Hunthausen was in Rome for his five-year bishop's visit and still pleading for an open investigation in Seattle.[35] He and other bishops were treated to Pope John extolling the proper role of women and the need to reaffirm church stands against contraception, divorce, homosexuality, premarital sex and abortion.[36] At that approximate set of minutes and hours, as hard to believe as it might sound, a U.S. Army Joint Logistics General stepped out of the darkness and asked me and some other officers, "Is anyone here from Montana?"[37]

I was just wiping my hands after helping an enlisted mechanic change out the engine in an armored Command Post Carrier.

"Yes, Sir."

"Where you from Captain?"

"I grew up in Butte, Miles City and the Bitterroot, but I'm from Helena now. Where you from, Sir?"

"Anaconda."

"Oh, then you must know "Dutch" Hunthausen!"

"Oh, yeah. My brother's working with a group out in Seattle that's about to take care of him."[38]

The general's sparse profanity and quiet tone left no doubt that a good man I still respect was about to face the storm of a lifetime.

NOTES

[5] Timothy P. Schilling, PhD dissertation, *Conflict in the Catholic Hierarchy: A Study of Coping Strategies in the Hunthausen Affair, with Preferential Attention to Discursive Strategies*, University of Utrecht, Netherlands, Appendix I: Chronology of the Rome-Hunthausen Case, igitur-archive.library.uu.nl/dissertations/2003-0206-111237/app.pdf

[6] Schilling's dissertation, page 148, Hickey's statement and Press Release.

[7] Carol M. Ostrom, "Vatican to Investigate Archbishop

Hunthausen," *The Seattle Times*, October 27, 1983, p. A-1.

[8] William Hartung, *Prophets of War, Lockheed Martin and the Making of the Military-Industrial Complex, Nation Books*, New York, NY, 2011, page 150.

[9] According to the Council of Trent, 1543-1545, "the principal object of all the visitations shall be to lead to sound and orthodox doctrine, by banishing heresies; to maintain good morals, and to correct such as are evil; to animate the people, by exhortations and admonitions, to religion, peacefulness, and innocence; and to establish such other things as to the prudence of the visitors shall seem for the profit of the faithful, according as time, place and opportunity shall allow." J. Waterworth, Editor, (1848 (1564)), *The Twenty-Fourth Session: Decree on Reformation, Chapter III, The Canons and Decrees of the Sacred and Ecumenical Council of Trent,* English translated from Latin. London: Dolman. Retrieved 5 December 2013.

[10] Carol M. Ostrom, "Is Probe a Blessing In Disguise?" *The Seattle Times,* November 5, 1983, page 13.

[11] Shilling dissertation chronology, page 354, indicates that Hickey had two assistants, but I've been able to identify only Father William Coyle, Redemptorist Chancellor to Bishop Justin Driscoll of the Diocese of Fargo, North Dakota.

[12] Schilling dissertation, page 200.

[13] Joseph Cardinal Ratzinger, Letter Closing the Apostolic Visitation Process, September 30, 1985, Sacred Congregation, *Seattle Catholic*, January 5, 2004, seattlecatholic.com/misc_20040105.html, says "at least 67." Shilling, in his dissertation, says "nearly 80."

[14] Schilling, at pages 102 & 105, discusses practical reasons why the Roman Catholic hierarchy employs secrecy.

[15] Ratzinger to Hunthausen, letter dated September 30, 1985.

[16] nytimes.com/1983/11/23/us/text-of-memorial-tribute-to-john-kennedy-in-the-capital-by-his-brother.html

[17] *Galveston Daily News,* November 23, 1983, newspaperarchive.com/galveston-daily-news/1983-11-23/page-2

[18] McFarlane to Reagan, Confidential Memorandum regarding Meeting with Vatican Secretary of State Agostino Cardinal Casaroli, November 22, 1983, Reagan Presidential Archives, Simi Valley, California

[19] Cobb to McFarlane, Confidential Memorandum, dated November 18, 1983, Reagan Presidential Archives, Simi Valley, California

[20] Gordon Thomas and Max Morgan-Witts, *The Year of Armageddon, The Pope and the Bomb,* Grenada, London, 1984, page 335.

[21] Ibid, page 336.

[22] Gregory Vistica, *Fall From Glory, the Men Who Sank the United States Navy,* Touchstone, New York, NY, 1995, page 150: "The American Knights (of Malta) disagreed not only with Hunthausen's anti-defense positions, but also with his stance on homosexuals and his liberal interpretations of church doctrine. They wanted him fired, and they were a formidable alliance."

[23] Barwig letter to Author, dated April 19th, 2011, page 1.

[24] Barwig to Reagan, dated November 24, 1983, and response, dated January 6, 1984, with White House staffing memorandum, dated December 19, 1983, from Tyrus Cobb to Robert Kimmitt, File 168373, Diplomatic Relations with the Vatican, Reagan Presidential Archives, Simi Valley, California

[25] Osborne to Darman, White House Memorandum, dated November 29, 1983, File 16837355, Diplomatic Relations with the Vatican, Ronald Reagan Presidential Archives, Simi Valley, California

[26] Schilling dissertation, page 129.

[27] Maria Luisa Ambrosini with Mary Willis, *The Secret Archives of the Vatican,* Barnes and Noble, 1969, pp. 5 & 6; "Co-located on the ground floor of the Secret Archives one can find records of the Consistory, an ecclesiastical senate of Cardinals that once as a body advised pope's on important matters, records of all conclaves that elected every pope since the time of Columbus, and the private archives of the Cardinals, which revert to the

church upon their death, or were purchased from their heirs."
[28] Large to Author, Email dated December 1, 2010; Ms. Ashley Large, Archivist for the Redemptorist Province of Denver wrote, "I'm sorry to have kept you waiting for these weeks, as I do not have good news regarding your request. I searched through Fr. Coyle's 18 boxes of materials only to find that we do not have anything regarding the Inquiry into Archbishop Hunthausen. This I find as odd and makes me think that these papers probably were taken completely out of the collection and accessioned elsewhere. Because they pertain to (arch) diocesan events, these documents may have been taken to either the Archdiocese of Seattle or the Diocese of Fargo. I cannot say this with certainty but perhaps these archives might be next in your search." Author's visit to Diocese of Fargo Offices found none of Father Coyle's papers.

[29] Dalby to Author, email, dated January 24, 2011. Seth Dalby, Archivist for the Archdiocese of Seattle, wrote: , "Unfortunately, I am not able to help you in this matter. Because the documents produced during this time record private and sensitive internal Church processes (and much personal information), this collection is closed to researchers" Author's Note: *The Code of Cannon Law* used to administer the Catholic Church devotes Canons 486 to 491 to the management of archives. Canon 489 states, "every diocese, which includes Rome, is to have a secret archive, or a safe or cabinet in the common archive, kept completely closed and locked, which cannot be removed; in it documents to be kept secret are to be protected most securely." According to Cannon 490, "only the bishop is to have the key to the secret archive. When a see is vacant, the secret archive or safe is not to be opened, except in a case of true necessity by the diocesan administrator himself. Documents are not to be removed from the secret archive or safe."
recordsjunkieblogspot.com/2009/05/archivists-catholic-archivists-and.html

[30] Schilling dissertation, page 147.

[31] John Allen, *National Catholic Reporter,* August 7, 2003, www.nationalcatholicreporter.org/updae/bn080703.htm

[32] I was serving as a Senior Armor Captain from the Montana Army National Guard's 163rd Armored Cavalry Regiment, individually detailed to the Operations Section of the U.S. Third Armored Cavalry Regiment, flown on a REFORGER 83 aircraft to Frankfurt, Germany, from Fort Bliss, Texas. We were the main effort of AUTUMN FORGE 83, and, according to the Soviets, who seem to have gotten the code names for our operations confused, the most dangerous of ABLE ARCHER 83.

[33] dw.de/remembering-inner-german-border-victims/a-16161679

[34] "Catholic gays pray in cathedral while protesters chant outside," *The Seattle Times,* September 6, 1983, page 42.

[35] Shilling dissertation timeline.

[36] "Pope speaks out on women's issues," *The Seattle Times,* September 6, 1983, page 6.

[37] qmfound.com/MG_William_McLean.htm

[38] General William "Tim" McLean to Author. The General doesn't now remember one of probably hundreds of such exchanges with lower ranking officers and enlisted personnel during his outstanding career.

CATHOLIC LEAGUE FOR RELIGIOUS AND CIVIL RIGHTS, 5-13-83
Brosnan, Stravinskas, Blum, President Reagan and Czajkowski

2. HOPE AND HUBRIS

The FBI office in Butte, Montana, opened the first internal security file on Hunthausen in May 1969 after the Priests' Senate of the Western Montana Diocese, supported by Hunthausen, took a stand against the Anti-Ballistic Missile System, calling it a dangerous escalation of the arms race and a huge waste of limited resources that could be used to help the poor.[39] From that time, Hunthausen would sometimes make his fellow prelates nervous with his openness to doctrinal change and protests against nuclear weapons, while becoming a visible and respected influence inside the U.S. National Conference of Catholic Bishops.[40] Together the U.S. Bishops struggled to establish moral standards regarding nuclear weapons. The Reagan Administration tried relentlessly to shape the ethical edge of U.S. Bishops' expected pastoral letter on war and peace in the nuclear age, *The Challenge of Peace.*[41] At the White House, two Catholics were on point. They were Judge William Clark, the President's National Security Advisor and close friend, and Dr. Chris Lehman, National Security Council Legislative Liaison and brother to Secretary of the Navy John F. Lehman.

Clark was the man pushing a long list of National Security Decision Directives, or NSDD, designed to put policy backbone behind presidential speeches that were building pressure on the Soviets. When Reagan called the Soviet Union an "Evil Empire" on March 8, 1983, he had signed NSDD 32, purposefully destabilizing the Polish government by all means necessary, and NSDD 75 making long-term spending on nuclear weapons our top national priority.[42] Fifteen days later, when Reagan declared that the U.S and U.S.S.R had reached parity or were even in nuclear war-fighting capability, he closed by saying:

> What if free people could live secure in the knowledge that their security did not rest upon the threat of instant U.S. retaliation to deter a Soviet attack; that we could intercept and destroy strategic ballistic missiles before they reached our own soil and that of our allies?

This speech introduced the Strategic Defense Initiative or SDI or "star wars" for its untried technology. Like a giant anti-ballistic missile system, the Soviets saw SDI leading to a first strike U.S. nuclear capability. Clark had been serving for eight months on the White House planning committee for SDI with two members of Reagan's kitchen cabinet, William Wilson and Joseph Coors. Clark handpicked Dr. Christopher Lehman as his aide, responsible for dealing with Milwaukee's Democrat Congressman Clement Zablocki, author of a house resolution proposing a Nuclear Freeze and another, HJR 316, enabling funding of a U.S. diplomatic mission to the Holy See. According to Dr. Lehman, during that 1982-1983 timeframe:

> The Bishops were the enemy.[43]

Both Catholic point men for U.S. National Security were unexpectedly absent from the November 23 White House meeting wrapping-up final arrangements for U.S. formal recognition of the Vatican. Clark didn't attend, because he had stepped down as National Security Advisor after Nancy Reagan sensed him driving her husband too far to the right.[44] Lehman didn't attend, because he was pre-occupied with staffing challenges stemming from KAL 007, the Kissinger Presidential Commission's October visit to Central America and the October 23 bombing of the U.S. Marine Barracks in Beirut. With all of this happening in the months leading up to formal recognition of the Vatican, there was no media coverage about opening full diplomatic channels to the Holy See.

As it happened, on December 31 our State Department tersely announced that formal diplomatic relations with the Holy See would commence at midnight. Ten days later the White House announced Reagan's intention to nominate his close friend Wilson to become the first U.S. Ambassador to the Holy See. On the same day as the White House press announcement, the Catholic League for Religious and Civil Rights, a non-profit non-church organization headquartered in Milwaukee, Wisconsin, issued it's own statement:

(Press Release) by Catholic League for Religious and Civil Liberties [sic] (Contact Anthony F. Czajkowski Ph.D. Telephone 202-737-4496). Regarding 'Ambassador to the Vatican.' President Reagan's nomination of William Wilson as ambassador to the Vatican is a major step towards the elimination of religious prejudice in the conduct of our nation's diplomatic affairs, according to the CLCRL. 'Diplomatically, the establishment of the relationship with the Vatican is routine business,' said Fr. Blum, 'but historically it is a great triumph that routine diplomatic business in the national interest can at last be openly conducted with the Vatican.' Fr. Blum noted that under the leadership of the late Congressman Clement Zablocki and Senator Richard Lugar an 1867 Law prohibiting the use of federal funds to support an American Embassy at the Vatican had been repealed last year, thus clearing the way for formal relations with the Vatican. Fr. Blum had earlier described the law as a 'Petty and childish symbol of religious bigotry and an unsavory relic of an era when the most blatant forms of anti-catholic prejudice were dominant in American politics.'

Though Father Virgil Blum's name was used throughout, it's striking that a Jesuit who founded the Catholic League in 1973 to serve as a "Catholic civil rights union, a Catholic Anti-defamation League," permitted Czajkowski to make this important public statement. Czajkowski, a Polish language speaker, first surfaced on behalf of the Catholic League in February 1979 when he signed into Congressman Zablocki's office as President of the Catholic League.[45] Zablocki was also a Polish language speaker and a close friend of Blum's. Zablocki's files hold numerous letters between "Virg" and "Clem." Jack Sullivan, a graduate student of Blum's and serving as Zablocki's Administrative Assistant and Legislative Assistant until 1976, confirmed that his teacher and his boss were friends.[46] The explanation for Blum's stepping to the background lies in Blum's files at Marquette's Archives. For the ten days after January 1, 1984, all of Blum's public utterances in Milwaukee were being reviewed by Father Vern Biever, a former Wisconsin Jesuit Provincial and Marquette University Vice President who had been assigned to the Catholic League. Blum appears to have avoided Biever's censorship by speaking through Czajkowski, a local chapter head half way across the country.

Blum's files indicate that in 1983 Czajkowski's was employed as a Contract Historian for the Central Intelligence Agency. The Air America aviation archives in Dallas at the University of Texas offer more information about Czajkowski.[47] In a 2004 audio taped interview, Czajkowski tells University of Georgia historian, Dr. William Leary, that before retiring in 1972 he had worked in the CIA for 20 years, rising to near the top of domestic U.S. intelligence operations. He turned U.S. tourists and exchange scientists into intelligence gatherers, authored the now declassified "Techniques of Domestic Intelligence Collection," and debriefed and found homes for pilots defecting from the eastern bloc.[48] Since he had a Doctorate in History from Fordham University, he says the CIA called him back into service in 1973 to compile and write a CIA history of Air America. He conducted interviews, took photographs and wrote 1,000 pages in twelve chapters before being ordered to kill the project. "They gave me three weeks to box it all up."[49] In keeping with the CIA doctrine or tradecraft which Czajkowski himself wrote, the experienced domestic intelligence operative would have sought to be Blum's confidante, later positioned to write and release a press release in place of Blum.

Czajkowski was two levels under Blum inside the Catholic League. His immediate boss was a young priest named Father Peter M.J. Stravinskas, who had no idea of Czajkowski's domestic intelligence background.[50] Stravinskas had his own role in the choreographed formal U.S. recognition of the Vatican. On February 2, 1984, he served as the American citizen testifying to the Senate Foreign Relations Committee in support of Wilson's confirmation as U.S. Ambassador to the Vatican. Interests opposed to Vatican recognition had been caught off guard on January 10 and proved unable to gain sufficient countering influence by February 21 when the U.S. Senate confirmed Wilson.[51] When Wilson presented his credentials at the Vatican, Archbishop Pio Laghi, Apostolic Delegate to the United States, became the new Papal Pro-Nuncio or Ambassador and presented his credentials at the White House. This improved status returned Laghi nearer to the full rank of Apostolic Nuncio he held in his previous assignment, where he played tennis weekly with Admiral Emilio Massera, one of Argentina's military junta during the dirty war. For another nine years, the title of Apostolic Nuncio would be reserved for Ambassadors from the Holy See who served as Deans of the entire corps of Ambassadors to a guest nation.

NOTES

[39] FBI response, dated October 19, 2011, to Freedom of

Information/Privacy Act (FOIPA No. 1164319-001), Subject: Hunthausen, Raymond G. (Archbishop): In the FBI office at Butte, Montana, someone placed the priests' statement, as reported in the May 8, 1969, *Montana Standard* in a file folder marked "Internal Security: Hunthausen."

[40] Author's interview of Archbishop Emeritus Eldon Curtis in Omaha, Nebraska.

[41] Richard Halloran, "U.S. Tells Bishops Morality is Guide on Nuclear Policy," *New York Times*, November 17, 1982.

[42] President Ronald Reagan, National Security Decision Directive 75, dated January 17, 1983.

[43] Author's interview of Dr. Chris Lehman in Clarendon, Virginia, May 30, 2013.

[44] Paul Kengore and Patricia Clark Doerner, *The Judge, William P. Clark, Ronald Reagan's Top Hand, Ignatius*, 2007, pp. 246-248.

[45] Congressman Zablocki's Invitations Pending Schedule for February 12, 1979, shows a meeting at 2:30 with Dr. Czajkowski, President of the Catholic League. There are no other mentions of the Catholic League in the entire period of Zablocki's records from 1973 until his death in 1983. Clement J. Zablocki Papers, Personal and Political Papers, PP-5, Box 1, Correspondence and Subject Files, 1936-1983, Marquette University Archives, Milwaukee, Wisconsin

[46] Sullivan to Author, Email dated April 23, 2011.

[47] McDonough Air Archives, University of Texas, Dallas, Texas.

[48] Anthony F. Czajkowski, "Techniques of Domestic Intelligence Collection," *Studies In Intelligence*, Volume 3, Winter, 1959, Classified CONFIDENTIAL, Approved for Release 1994 *CIA Historical Review Program*; foia.cia.gov/sites/default/files/document_conversions/89801/DOC_0000607343.pdf

[49] William P. Leary Papers, University of Texas-Dallas, Special Collections, Sub-Series 21, Box 81, Folder 34, Audio-Tape, Czajkowski, August 13, 1994, McDonough Air Archives, University of Texas, Dallas, Texas.

[50] Author's interview with Father Peter M.J. Stravinskas in Toms River, New Jersey.

[51] csmonitor.com/1984/0213/021346.html

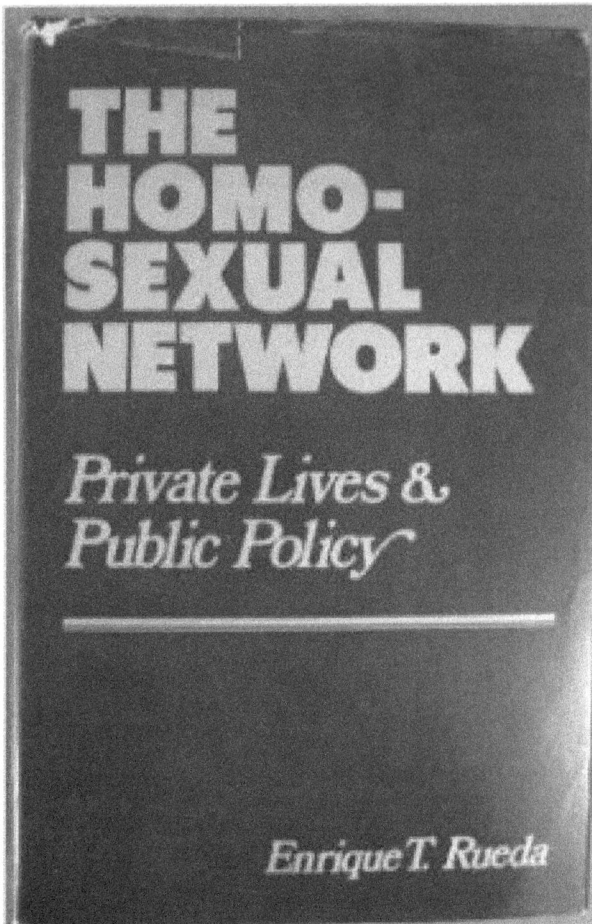

THE HOMO-SEXUAL NETWORK

Private Lives & Public Policy

Enrique T. Rueda

LABELS

3. VILE PROPAGANDA

"Laghi played tennis every day with Bush. They were neighbors," were the first words from Stravinskas upon learning of Czajkowski's extensive CIA domestic intelligence background. In December after Reagan's 1980 election, Casaroli posted Laghi to the U.S. where he had previously served in the Apostolic Delegation. Stravinskas, working on the East Coast, had been with the Catholic League for more than year. Previously he served as Chaplain at Bishop Kelly High School in Boise, Idaho. Stravinskas' irritation with Hunthausen's doctrinal casualness dates from then:

> The man is a heretic.[52] He was running a protestant archdiocese out there. [Apostolic Delegate Archbishop] Jadot should never have appointed him. It was incredible what was going on out there in both the Diocese of Helena and the Archdiocese of Seattle . . . There was already a body of complaints from priests and religious in Laghi's office. John Paul knew about this. [53]

Stravinskas, who thinks the Jesuits in the U.S. run pagan universities, remembers the tense-muscled look of anger that swept his friend Laghi's face during a U.S. Bishop's meeting as Chicago's Cardinal Bernardin unexpectedly opened a discussion about the Vatican's treatment of Hunthausen. Stravinskas had known Laghi for some time after working as staff coordinator for the Catholic League 10th Anniversary Celebration. As part of that celebration, Apostolic Delegate Laghi attended a May 21, 1983, Solemn Papal High Mass at New York's Saint Patrick's Cathedral and a dinner following at the Waldorf-Astoria Hotel. Hickey celebrated in Washington D.C. with a Mass at the Shrine of the Immaculate Conception. Because Reagan couldn't make the New York City fete, Stravinskas arranged through the Apostolic Delegation for himself, Blum, Czajkowski and economist Anne Brosnan, Secretary of the Catholic League, to meet at the White House with the President on May 13 to award him their "Pope John Paul II Religious Freedom Award." The White House Staff notes indicate their point of contact on the Apostolic Delegation Staff was a young American priest, Father Blase Cupich.[54] During the meeting in the White House, Reagan asked Stravinskas and Blum to stay behind for a chat during which Blum complained about the failure of public funding for Catholic schools. According to Stravinskas, Reagan calmed him saying:

> I'm not your enemy Father. Your enemy is the National Conference of Catholic Bishops.[55]

During this time Michael Schwartz, the Catholic League's Director of Public Affairs, stayed busy on another broad front.

Blum's files indicate that after June 9, 1981, the Jesuit mentor had lost positive control over Schwartz's remarkable industriousness.[56] After a December 15, 1994, interview, investigative journalist Gregory Vistica reported, "Michael Schwartz, a conservative Catholic close to many prominent Republicans, helped coordinate the effort [to initiate an Apostolic Visitation of Seattle Archbishop Hunthausen by the Holy See] in the United States and noted with some pride that much of the Reagan administration's national security apparatus was composed of conservative Catholics." Both Schwartz and Stravinskas separately said, "Blum strictly forbid us from getting involved in the internal workings of the church." Though Schwartz didn't recall being interviewed by Vistica, he did not deny its content, and he suggested: "Maybe" the Apostolic Visitation landed on Hunthusen "because of his high profile."[57]

Just after the Catholic League's big anniversary celebration, Blum learned from a note on the bulletin board in Marquette's Jesuit Residence that Father Biever would be assigned to the Catholic League. Not realizing that Biever would censor him, Blum was ecstatic about a possible Jesuit successor and told this to his staff:

> Because I too think it is a fact that the Catholic Laity still, much to my regret, psychologically need the leadership of the clergy, I have been talking with my Father Provincial, Father Joe Labaj, for the last two years about assigning another Jesuit to the Catholic League. Such an assignment was made yesterday.[58]

Catholic League Board Chairman Dr. James Hitchcock remembers questioning Blum about Biever's leanings, apparent from his book *Religion, Culture and Values*.[59] He also remembers tension quickly developing between Biever and Schwartz concerning the latter's statements on abortion. Hitchcock had no idea that Biever was censoring Blum or that he'd expressed objections about Hitchcock's own public positions for the Catholic League.[60] According to Blum, Schwartz soon started "freelancing."[61]

Continuing as Director of Public Relations, Schwartz completed *The Persistent Prejudice, Anti-Catholicism in America*, which conveys many of Blum's stock ideas, such as treating arguments based upon separation of church and state as code for "anti-Catholicism."[62] In 1984, Blum abruptly asked for Stravinskas' resignation without informing his Board of Directors,[63] and in 1986, Schwartz left the Catholic League to serve as Director of Paul Weyrich's Catholic Center, which was then publishing Father Enrique Rueda's monograph *The Marxist Character of Liberation Theology*. In 1987, Schwartz and Rueda co-authored *Gays, Aids and You*.

Weyrich was a prominent Republican and a conservative Melkite Catholic who founded the Heritage Foundation using money from Coors.[64] After accomplishing the Heritage Foundation, Weyrich used more money from Coors in the 1980s to create the Free Congress Research and Education Foundation.[65] In late June 1981, Weyrich appointed Cuban-born Rueda to be the first Director for a new entity called the Catholic Center for Free Enterprise, Strong Defense and Traditional Values. A few days earlier Hunthausen had spoken in Tacoma about the moral imperative for Christians to disarm themselves of nuclear weapons non-violently. He based his conclusions on Christian teaching from the gospel, as he shared his thoughts with a convention of gathered Lutherans. He argued for disarmament as a step toward addressing larger questions of public morality, despair and violence in our society. He suggested the most effective strategy is one of non-violence, like the one in which he was participating against the nearby Trident missile submarine base at Bangor, Washington. In the speech, he used the moral metaphor of Bangor, Washington, as an Auschwitz in Puget Sound. He foretold that persecution would be a consequence of peacemaking but called unilateral disarmament the cross Christians must bear in the nuclear age. He called for non-violent action.[66] Hunthausen then elaborated on the notion of withholding some tax payments to a government that relentlessly devotes more than half of every tax dollar to war-making capability. This part of his speech caused the greatest stir.

In Washington D.C., Weyrich formed the new Catholic Center a few days after Hunthausen's speech. Its Director Rueda would:

> . . . focus on a new and disquieting phenomenon: The progressive movement to the Left by important social structures within the [Catholic] church.[67]

Rueda, ordained a Catholic priest after coming to the states, was, according to his brother, in desperate need of money to support his refugee siblings and aging parents.[68] Having earned a couple of degrees, he worked as a Research Fellow for Weyrich. Since April 1980, Rueda researched and wrote, with no peer reviewer except Weyrich, a 680-page monograph about "the social and political impact of the homosexual movement in America."[69] In it Rueda formally invented the word "prohomosexual" and created a list of sixteen prohomosexual Catholic bishops by compiling their names from statements each made empathizing with homosexuals. He took their statements from what he called the "Catholic prohomosexual center New Ways Ministry" booklet, "A Collection of Contemporary Statements from U.S. Catholic Sources on Homosexuality, Gay Ministry and Social Justice." He made a shorter list of seven prohomosexual Catholic bishops based on names mentioned in another New Ways Ministry article. Both lists featured Hunthausen's name emphasized by Rueda for having written a letter in support of efforts to pass legislation "granting privileges to homosexuals" in the State of Washington. Rueda noted, "This letter, dated July 1, 1977, seems to coincide with Gay Pride Week." In the middle of his book asserting a homosexual threat, Rueda described Hunthausen's protests against the Trident missiles:

> Hunthausen has become something of a cause celebre for the New Left. He participated in a demonstration against the Trident submarine at a military installation, which has been the object of leftist demonstrations since 1976. On

June 12, 1981, Archbishop Hunthausen, speaking to six hundred delegates at the Pacific Lutheran Convention of the Lutheran Church of America in Tacoma, called upon Christians to refuse to pay a substantial portion of their federal income taxes in protests against American defense efforts.[70]

In March 1982 the *Wall Street Journal* reported that the Catholic Center's purpose was to generate enough significant negative publicity for Catholic bishops to make them "squeal and squirm in anguish."[71] By October, Weyrich published Rueda's monograph as *The Homosexual Network, Private Lives and Public Policy.*[72] On October 10, Rueda arrived at the Vatican with Wilson's help.[73] It was no secret that Ratzinger and Pope John Paul II both condemned homosexuality.[74] Like blue dye revealing a surreptitious network to the highest ranking staff office of the Roman Curia, Rueda's new word pro-homosexual, hyphenated by an English-speaking editor somewhere in the Vatican, appeared in Seattle in Ratzinger's September 30, 1985, letter closing the Apostolic Visitation.[75] By then the Catholic Center had also tried through Wilson's office to influence Pope John Paul II against the U.S. Bishops pastoral letter on Catholic Social teachings and the U.S. Economy.[76] Weyrich's Catholic Center wanted the new U.S. Ambassador at the Vatican to arrange an audience for Catholic congressmen to be able to ask the Pope to read Rueda's subsequent monograph, *Roman Catholicism and American Capitalism, Friends or Foes?*.

NOTES

[52] The definition of "heresy" is "holding a belief or opinion contrary to orthodox religious doctrine."

[53] Author's interview with Father Peter M.J. Stravinskas in Toms River, New Jersey,

[54] Blum to Reagan, Catholic League Letter dated March 23, 1983, included with White House Staff, Faith Whittlesey's Memorandum regarding the planned Oval Office meeting. Describes the Catholic

League as a "grassroots," volunteer, private initiative group with no connection to the "official" (Catholic) Church establishment. The League has 26,000 contributing members and is governed by a largely lay board." Reagan Presidential Archives, Simi Valley, California

[55] Stravinskas interview.

[56] Schwartz to Blum, typed periodic report contains proposals for writing, press contacts and meetings with chapters; Blum approved scholarly writing for *Commentary*, establishing contacts with Spanish-Americans and Knights of Columbus, and insisted Schwartz record his telephone conversations for Blum's review.

[57] Author's interview of Michael Schwartz in Washington, D.C., April 13, 2012.

[58] Father Virgil Blum, S.J. notes ("Rationale for another priest on the staff of the Catholic League for Religious and Civil Rights"), dated July 21, 1983, for Staff Meeting of the Catholic League for Religious and Civil Rights. Blum's papers, Marquette University Archives, Milwaukee, Wisconsin.

[59] Hitchcock to Blum, letter dated September 9, 1983.

[60] Biever to Blum, letter dated February 10, 1984; Hitchcock to Author, Email dated April 7, 2011: "Now you have enlightened me. I had no idea that Biever was censoring Blum, but it all makes sense. Biever was an ex-SJ provincial, and it was a mystery as to why he "lowered himself" to work for Blum. Now it appears that the SJ put him in order to ride herd on Blum. There was tension between Biever and Schwartz, because Biever thought S. exaggerated the abortion issue. I resigned from the board in 1985 (?) because I thought Blum was mismanaging the CL – staff had become a revolving door, and he had tensions with just about everybody. Now I wonder if Biever was behind that. (You can quote anything I say in these emails)."

[61] Blum to Young, letter, dated April 14, 1986, regarding Emile Comar's internal investigation of Catholic League during August 2-4, 1985: "Mike is a very talented man writes and speaks well, is very ideological, and was a good ambassador of the Catholic

League as Director of Public Affairs. As a native Philadelphian, he never adjusted to life in the Middle West and continually agitated for moving the national office of the Catholic League to Washington. Moreover, during his last two years with the league (August 83-85), he spent most of his time on the road for television and radio appearances and press conferences. When at home, he was almost continually engaged in telephone conversations or at the typewriter. During these years Mike was a freelancer, doing what he wanted to do and traveling where he wanted to go."

[62] Michael Schwartz, *The Persistent Prejudice, Anti-Catholicism in America,* Our Sunday Visitor, Inc, Huntington, Indiana, 1984.

[63] Reporter Joseph Sobran surveyed the Catholic League staff situation for *The Wanderer*, a lay Catholic newspaper. Stravinskas told reporter Sobran, "I feel my performance over five years is a matter of public record and I think that record is credible. That surely was the understanding of a number of persons who wrote me after my resignation, including bishops, Jewish leaders with who I have worked, Curial officials in Rome, and others." Sobran then asked, "Curial officials?" The 34-year old priest responded, "Archbishop Paul Marcinkus (Third in Command of the Vatican State) and Cardinal-designate Edouard Gagnon (Canadian Vice Chancellor of the Pontifical College and President of the Pontifical Council for the Family)."

[64] Dan Baum, *Citizen Coors, An American Dynasty,* William Morrow, New York, NY, 2000, page 345.

[65] Ed Feulner, President of the Heritage Foundation, "R.I.P. Paul Weyrich" in the *National Review,* December 18, 2008, nationalreview.com/corner/174966/r-i-p-paul-weyrich/ed-feulner

[66] Archbishop Raymond G. Hunthausen, "Controlling Nuclear Arms with Non-Violence," Tacoma, Washington, June 12, 1981.

[67] Enrique T. Rueda, *Roman Catholicism and American Capitalism: Friends or Foes?* The Catholic Center for Free Enterprise, Strong Defense and Traditional Values of the Free Congress Research and Education Foundation, 1984, page iii.

[68] Authors interview of Mr. Guillermo C. Rueda, Father Rueda's brother, by telephone while in Little Havana, Miami, Florida.

[69] Enrique Rueda, *The Homosexual Network, Private Lives and Public Policy,* Devin Adair Company Old Greenwich, CT, 1982. "I do not advocate persecution of homosexuals or their condemnation on account of their condition. I do not advocate anything. I accept homosexuals as human beings and children of God, entitled to our love and concern, and God's love as much as anyone else. If the reader is seeking enlightenment on the value of homosexual behavior, he will not find it here. Homosexuality is a manifestation of the sinful condition that affects mankind and each man, and homosexual behavior is gravely sinful by the very nature of the reality. I'm fully committed to the proposition that homosexuals should not be entitled to special treatment under the law. That would be tantamount to rewarding evil. Given that America's traditional religious beliefs have always condemned the practice of homosexuality and social convention has reduced mention of the subject to a minimum, it's clear that a revolution has taken place in the last thirty years. There is a homosexual movement, intent upon infiltrating liberal organizations and the Catholic Church. I base this conclusion on my belief that there is a homosexual ideology as follows: There's a distinction between Gay and Homosexual: Gay is good; and, Coming out is desirable. There are a large number of Homosexuals constituting a legitimate minority. Homosexuality in itself has no moral implications, and is not a matter of choice, not changeable and not an illness. The homosexual ideology is revolutionary in nature, and homophobia is an undesirable condition. The ultimate goal of the homosexual movement is acceptance of homosexual acts as a normal variant of human behavior and of homosexuality as an alternative lifestyle. The homosexual movement fully intends to make the homosexualization of American schools a key component in its overall plan to mold our nation in its image and likeness. Whether it is successful depends not only on the skill and determination of the homosexual leaders

and their allies, but on the resolve of parents to gain control over the educational system. In this work the new word, "prohomosexual," means promoting conditions favorable to the practice of homosexuality, or a principle of the homosexual ideology, as proposed by various homosexual sources."

[70] Ibid.

[71] John J. Fialka, "Atom-Weapons Issue Stirs Divisive Debate in the Catholic Church," *Wall Street Journal,* June 9, 1982 (Footnote from Penny Lernoux, *People of God, the Struggle for World Catholicism,* Viking, New York, NY, 1989, page 175).

[72] Enrique Rueda, *The Homosexual Network, Private Lives and Public Policy,* Devin Adair Company Old Greenwich, CT, 1982.

[73] Wilson to Hornblower Telex, dated September 23, 1982, Special Collections Archives, Georgetown University, Washington, D.C. "Fr. Enrique Rueda is meeting me in Washington on Monday, September 27, in the State Department, but he has requested a ticket for the canonization on Oct. 10 and I would appreciate it if you would make these arrangements for him. Bob Smolik knows his address and telephone number in Washington and can reach him to tell him when you have tickets for him, if you will so inform him."

[74] Jonathan Kwitny, *Man of the Century, The Life and Times of Pope John Paul II*, Holt and Company, New York, NY, 1997, pp. 165-166, 339, 570.

[75] Ratzinger to Hunthausen, letter dated September 30, 1985, paragraph 14.

[76] usccb.org/upload/economic_justice_for-all.pdf

CARDINALS

4. COMPROMISED HIERARCHY

Weyrich's reputable admirers say his usual strategy was "to act as an outside vehicle either to mobilize grassroots support behind legislative initiatives, or to coordinate strategies to defeat liberal initiatives."[77] Purposeful or not, Rueda's listing techniques, the same as those used in Castro's Cuba to target people for prison, served the same purpose as the lists right-wing extremists in the U.S. used to target Jewish-American talk show host Allen Berg for assassination. Berg died in a hail of bullets in his Denver, Colorado, driveway as he stepped out of his car.[78] In the same way, Hunthausen was being set up for character assassination by "truth squads" sent to Seattle to make the archbishop's pastoral positions appear in a bad light. Rueda quickly became popular leading workshops in Seattle with participants from the mailing list of *The Wanderer*, which was critical of pastoral American bishops for what it perceived as their "liberalism." Rueda damned Liberation Theology as Marxist, and he suggested that groups associated with Liberation Theology, including Maryknoll missionaries and Brazilian bishops, were "part of a subversive movement led by the Soviet Union." After studying Rueda's practices, Penny Lernoux concluded that he intended to make troublemakers of workshop participants, getting them to circulate petitions, write letters to the Vatican, publish newspaper advertisements, discourage church donations and otherwise harass bishops. He would assure attendees "the Vatican is telling us to do this."[79]

At least three different organizations popped up in the Seattle Archdiocese doing these sorts of things. Writer and columnist, Mr. Erven Park of Kelso, Washington, organized and led the Northwest Laity for Truth, a Wanderer Forum affiliate, peppering the Vatican with letters.[80] Park called Hunthausen a "subversive," edited a newsletter called *The Catholic Truth* and took pride in the fact that he provided one of the secret papal depositions to the Apostolic Visitation.[81] Danny Barrett of Des Moines, Washington, organized and led the Catholics United Against Marxist Theology,[82] critical of Hunthausen's position against armaments. Retired attorney, William Gaffney of Seattle organized and led Catholics United By Faith. Later when the Vatican tried to remove some of Hunthausen's authority, Gaffney, whose organization "had been writing letters to the Vatican for years complaining of the Archbishop's ministry," applauded the power-sharing move of Coadjutor Bishop Donald Wuerl into the Seattle chancery as "reasonable and necessary."[83] The wave of complaints from the Seattle area crested in January 1983 with a specific letter about what is known as the "balloon funeral."[84]

This incident, highlighted by *Time* magazine's coverage of the November 1983 Apostolic Visitation, took place at St. Michael's Church in Olympia, Washington.[85] A mother, distraught enough to determine who should be contacted on the Pope's staff in the Vatican, described her son's funeral conducted by Father Paul Dalton. In his remarks to the gathered mourners, Dalton mentioned that the man's own wife, the mother's daughter-in-law, performed an otherwise priestly function by anointing her dying husband during the Sacrament of Extreme Unction, or Last Rites. The funeral celebration included her daughter dressed as a clown pirouetting and tying inflated balloons to the casket that was then placed in her son's pickup truck by pall-bearers wearing work shirts. This letter is the one thought to have given Ratzinger his technical reason for an Apostolic Visitation.

Ratzinger came to this decision as Hunthausen and the other U.S. Bishops were grappling with the Reagan Administration about final ethical guidance on nuclear war.[86] During that process, extending from early 1982 through May 1983, Clark, who visited with Pope John Paul II more than Reagan did, tried to get the U.S. Bishops to back the Reagan Administration's three nuclear arms control initiatives.[87] On March 4, 1982, he directed national security cabinet members to address issues raised by the U.S. Bishops, by writing:

> The Archbishops' Committee is preparing a report for the National Conference, which could result in a declaration that a strategy of deterrence is immoral. The implications of such a declaration are obvious.

With an open letter on November 22, he tried one last time to change their minds. Then on February 8, 1983, he handed a classified brief to Laghi, a foreign national, rather than sharing it with America's own bishops.[88] Laghi and Casaroli ingratiated themselves by bringing members of the U.S. Bishops' Peace Pastoral Committee to Rome for meetings. By then, Clark and CIA Director William Casey were regularly visiting Laghi's residence, and Laghi frequently entered the White House through a side door to meet with Clark.[89]

Clark remained in close contact with Wilson, who finally got an appointment to talk with Ratzinger. On Tuesday, March 22, 1983, State Department Foreign Service Officer Michael

Hornblower, working the Vatican desk at the U.S. Embassy in Rome, telexed Wilson:

> You have an appointment Monday [March 28, 1983] at 11 with Silvestrini and at 12:15 with Ratzinger. Casaroli is difficult until after Easter [April 3].[90]

Wilson would have legitimate reason to try and influence Archbishop Achille Silvestrini, the man handling the war in Nicaragua for John Paul II. There was no acceptable reason for Wilson to be trying to influence Ratzinger, the supposed centralized keeper of every Catholic's Faith. There may have been other meetings, but this message is the only document among Wilson's papers, proving that someone from the Reagan Administration met with Ratzinger. The evident meeting happened two months after Ratzinger received the balloon funeral letter and a month before the U.S. Bishops were to meet in Chicago for a final vote on the *Challenge of Peace*. The only subject the two men had in common to discuss would have been the pending ethical guidance and the prominence of Archbishop Hunthausen. Wilson, a convert to Catholicism, had the title "Ambassador Faux Pas," because he was candid enough to convince the Vatican that something dramatic needed to be done about a likeable guy like Hunthausen.[91]

Being a U.S. Ambassador to the Holy See was Wilson's highest personal goal, and the Vatican diplomatic corps, oldest in the world, wanted formal diplomatic recognition from the U.S. Wilson would have learned from Ratzinger about the pending Apostolic Visitation before it became a Papal Secret. Though not the sort of person to blab about something that important, he would have passed word of the reassuring disciplinary action back to Clark. Thirty-six days later the U.S. National Conference of Catholic Bishops gave only general support to the initiatives of the Reagan Administration. They conditioned their approval of nuclear deterrence as a sufficiently moral reason for nuclear weapons, only as a step toward abolishing them.[92] At that meeting, Laghi, who had already been in the U.S. for 30 months, surprised and pleased Hunthausen with his announcement that there would be an Apostolic Visitation.[93] Clark would have passed to his handpicked aide, Lehman, his certain knowledge that this highest profile of the U.S. Bishops would be receiving some sort of discipline.[94] Lehman had the key chop, or review and approval responsibility, on an early August 1983 U.S. National Security Council Action Memorandum to Clark from Peter Sommers, recommending approval of a statement about formally recognizing the Vatican.[95]

The Catholic Lehman brothers, one at the National Security Council and one at Navy, were close. By 1983 they had already joined efforts to retain the phrase "maritime superiority" in Reagan's speeches. It maintained the strategic rationale for spending huge amounts of money on naval expansion. They also joined forces to cause a premature release of a White House press statement naming two aircraft carriers, the Abraham Lincoln and the George Washington, thereby out-maneuvering Navy brass who were in the process of trimming the defense budget to one carrier with its extensive support requirements.[96] Secretary of Navy Lehman had already made clear his strong antipathy toward Hunthausen during a March 8, 1982, speech at the Temple of the Four Chaplains in Philadelphia.

The mysterious leak on the U.S. East Coast that forced Archbishops Hickey and Hunthausen to reveal the existence of the Apostolic Visitation in Seattle would have seeped to Navy Secretary Lehman from his brother, who got it from Clark, who got it from Wilson's report of his meeting with Ratzinger.

NOTES

[77] Edwin J. Feulner, Jr., *The Story of the Republican Study Committee,* The Kingston Group, 1983, page 210.
[78] denverpost.com/commented/ci_12615628
[79] Lernoux, *The People of God,* pp. 173-74.
[80]seattlecatholic.com/nwlaity/articleBrunettLetter01.html; articles.latimes.com/1986-12-20/news/ss-4391_1_father-

matthew-fox/2;
people.com/people/archives/article/0,,20095304,00.html
[81] Note at bottom of essay in seattlecathollic.com/a051005.html
[82] nytimes.com/1985/11/28/us/pst-of-seattle-archbishop-is-affirmed-by-vatican-after-an-inquiry.html
[83] nytimes.com/1986/09/06/us/vatican-change-in-seattle-protested.html
[84] Gordon Thomas and Max Morgan-Witts, pp. 333-337.
[85] "Checking up on Dutch," Time, November 28, 1983, content.time.com/time/magazine/article/0.9171/926406/00.html
[86] Following the bishops' November, 1980, general meeting, a committee of bishops was appointed to draft a pastoral letter on war and peace. The first draft of this letter was submitted to the bishops in June 1982, with subsequent drafts presented in November 1982 and May 1983. Approval of the text by the body of bishops was given during the plenary assembly in Chicago on May 3, 1983, old.usccb.org/sdwp/international/TheChallengeofPeace.pdf
[87] Kengor and Derner, page 171; Clark to Bernadin, letter dated November 16, 1982, nuclearfiles.org/menu/key-issues/ethics/issues/religious/clark-archbishop-bernadin_print.htm
[88] Laghi to Clark, Personal and Confidential Letter, dated February 9, 1983, Bishops' letters-October 1982 (4), Box 90745, Richard C. Morris File, Reagan Presidential Archives, Simi Valley, California: "Dear Judge Clark: With gratitude I wish to acknowledge your letter of February 8, 1983 and the confidential report which you enclosed. For your information, I have made this material available to my superiors and wish to assure you that the notation of secrecy will be respected. With kind regards, I remain, Sincerely yours, Pio Laghi Apostolic Delegate;"
[89] Carl Bernstein, "The Holy Alliance," Time, February 24, 1992, carlbernstein.com/magazine_holy _alliance.php
[90] Hornblower to Wilson Telex dated March 22, 1983, Special Collections Archives, Georgetown University, Washington, D.C.

[91] Peter S. Bridges, Deputy Chief of Mission, Rome, 1981-1984, Interview by Charles Stuart Kennedy October 24, 2003, The Association for Diplomatic Studies and Training, Foreign Affairs Oral History Project, Holy See Country Reader, adst.org/Readers/Holy%20See.pdf

[92] National Council of Catholic Bishops, *The Challenge of Peace: God's Promise and Our Response, A Pastoral Letter on War and Peace,* May 3, 1983, old.usccb.org/sdwp/international/TheChallengeofPeace.pdf

[93] Author's interview of Father Michael Ryan, former Seattle Archdiocese Chancellor, in Seattle April 20, 2011.

[94] John F. Lehman, Jr., *Command of the Seas,* Naval Institute Press, Annapolis, MD, 1988, footnote at page 150.

[95] Sommer to Clark, National Security Council Action Memorandum, dated August 10, 1983; Subject: Diplomatic Relations with the Vatican, Chris Lehman and Don Fortier, concurring, File 165395, Reagan Presidential Archives, Simi Valley, California

[96] These incidents of fraternal cooperation in the national security policy environment have been mentioned in at least three different books by authors Vistica, Paztor and Smith, respectively.

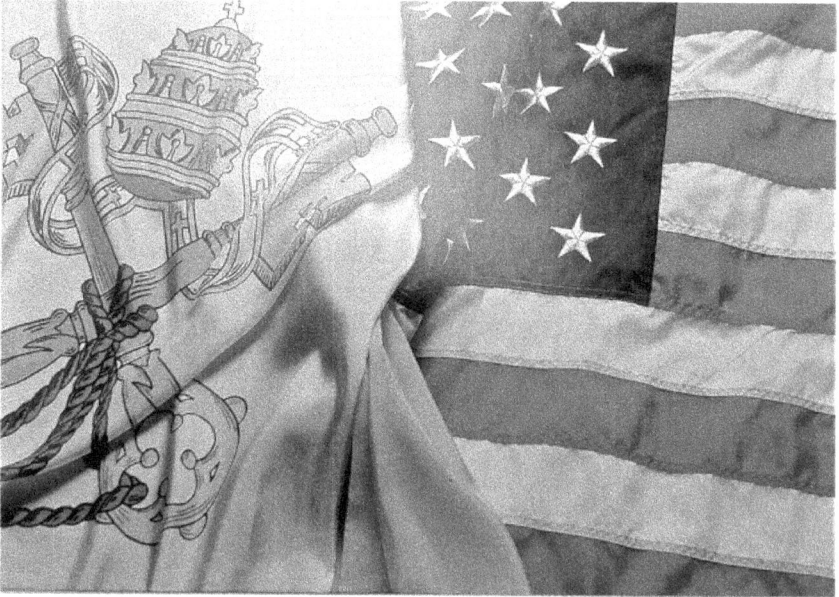

U.S. FORMAL RECOGNITION OF THE HOLY SEE

5. AN ARDENT CONVERT

Wilson, like it or not, deserves full credit for formal U.S. diplomatic recognition of the Holy See, because he and his staff worked closely with both houses of Congress, the U.S. State Department and the National Security Staff in the White House to make recognition a reality. According to a comment Wilson made to a Foreign Service Officer, even Reagan had to be convinced of the value of diplomatic ties by Queen Elizabeth. After the November 1980 election, Wilson headed the Reagan kitchen cabinet's Presidential Personnel Selection Committee, screening applicants for high positions in the new administration. He offered himself to be Reagan's Personal Envoy to the Holy See, both men thinking it was like any other ambassador's job. In an October 30, 1981, letter to Senator Charles Percy, Wilson wrote:

. . . the President was under the impression that the post was equivalent to a full ambassadorship and I think he believed the office had a status accorded a fully accredited embassy. When I returned from my first visit to Rome I was able to brief him on the facts as they are.

Wilson also told Percy about an article appearing in the October 27, 1981, *New York Post* and titled "Reagan Stepping Up Ties to the Vatican":

> I was absolutely flabbergasted. There is little, if any, factual substance behind it. I have discussed this matter with you, with Senator Helms and with Judge Clark and that is the limit of my discussions on this subject with anyone in Washington. The issue was raised in the Vatican in my final meeting there last week, but there is no way that I can conceive that they would have discussed this matter outside the Vatican.[97]

Then he suggested using the leak as a trial balloon for gauging public reaction to the idea.

Wilson thought constantly of formal recognition. A professional diplomat working in Rome recalled that Wilson wanted to be a real ambassador on a par with Max Rabb, U.S. Ambassador to Italy. Yet, spending only 20 weeks a year in Europe made Wilson seem scattered and blunt. This became most obvious in June 1981 while attending the huge funeral mass of Joseph Cardinal Wyzinski, leader of Poland's parallel government. Wilson was one of the five-member U.S. Delegation led by Zablocki, flying in a plane marked United States of America. With the plane as backdrop, Philadelphia's Polish-American Cardinal John Krol delivered, in Polish, the delegation's carefully crafted statement to prime time Warsaw Television. But later, when Solidarity's leader Lech Walesa suggested that there would soon be investment flowing to Poland from U.S. business, Wilson reacted:

> Well, how is that? Is it because you're so free of strikes? Is it because your independence is so secure?[98]

Using indirect means, Wilson eventually dug himself out of that hole and gained Zablocki's support by supporting the Congressman as he led his delegation to the Vatican. Wilson also worked members of the House Foreign Affairs Committee through Hornblower and Vatican counterparts. The professional diplomats saw to it that Zablocki's delegation received the highest possible level of VIP attention, especially from Pope John Paul II who awarded Zablocki the Order of Saint Gregory the Great. On February 21, 1983, State Department Executive Secretary L. Paul Bremer, III passed this inside information about the Vatican's action from the State Department to Clark.[99] Clark told staff member John Poindexter to get news of the award to Reagan in California. Poindexter noted:

> We feel it would help with [stopping] the nuclear freeze issue.[100]

Reagan's congratulatory note, signed by autopen, left the White House May 2.[101] Hornblower could see that Zablocki and committee were coming around to support the idea of funding a U.S. Vatican Embassy and he telexed:

> "What are we waiting for?"

No congressional staff working for Zablocki, including George Berdes, Ivo Spalatin and Legislative Assistant Gail Amidzich, recalls working on a resolution enabling Vatican recognition.[102] On June 30, Zablocki and 35 members of the House Foreign Affairs Committee introduced HJR 316, removing restrictions on funding a U.S. Diplomatic Mission to the Holy See. At the State Department, Bremer prepared an analysis for the White House about a proposed State Department public statement on HJR 316 and reminded all to emphasize that formal recognition of the Vatican was a congressional initiative. Yet, there was little if any press attention. On July 17, one short newspaper article, based on highly placed congressional sources, noted that positive signals had come from the White House regarding Vatican relations.[103]

To gain the support of the U.S. Senate Foreign Relations Committee, Wilson had been working through Patrick Ballistieri, a committee staff person. On July 21, Ballistieri reported to Wilson that Senator Richard Lugar asked his colleagues to support a bill lifting the Congressional prohibition against funding a U.S.

Embassy at the Vatican.[104] That bill, introduced on July 27, mirrored Zablocki's. Then Zablocki's House Foreign Affairs Committee combined the bill with HR 2915, an already committee-approved Department of State Authorization which received Reagan's signature November 22, that day of informal brushes with Casaroli and Laghi.[105] After the November 23 wrap-up meeting with Casaroli in the White House, Reagan told his staff and the State Department to act normally, so as not to attract attention to cable exchanges.

On December 3, Zablocki died from a heart attack suffered at night in his office.[106] With that, his Nuclear Freeze Resolution opposed by the White House floated into Senate limbo, leaving Navy Secretary Lehman's Assistant Secretary for Research, Engineering and Systems, Melvyn Paisley, free to continue massively expanding the Trident nuclear missile submarine fleet.[107] Lehman would have already passed to Paisley the inside news that Hunthausen was about to be quieted.

NOTES

[97] William A. Wilson to Senator Charles Percy, letter dated October 30, 1981, Special Collections Archives, Georgetown University, Washington D.C.

[98] Bridges' Oral History Interview.

[99] Bremer to Clark, Department of State Memorandum, dated February 21, 1983, Reagan Presidential Archives, Simi Valley, California

[100] Poindexter to Duberstein, White House Memorandum, dated March 1, 1983, Reagan Presidential Archives, Simi Valley, California

[101] Ibid.

[102] Email Spalatin to Driscoll, dated April 26, 2011.

[103] Susanne Schafer, Associated Press, "Reagan Seen Open to Setting Up Diplomatic Links with the Vatican," *The Buffalo News*, July 17, 1983.

[104] Letter William A. Wilson to Patrick Ballistieri, dated July 29,

1983, Special Collections Archives, Georgetown University, Washington, D.C.

[105] Roberts to Fielding, White House Memorandum, dated November 21, 1983, Reagan Presidential Archives, Simi Valley, California

[106] Steven V. Roberts, "Clement J. Zablocki of Foreign Affairs Panel Dies," *New York Times*, December 3, 1983.

[107] Vistica, pp. 164-166.

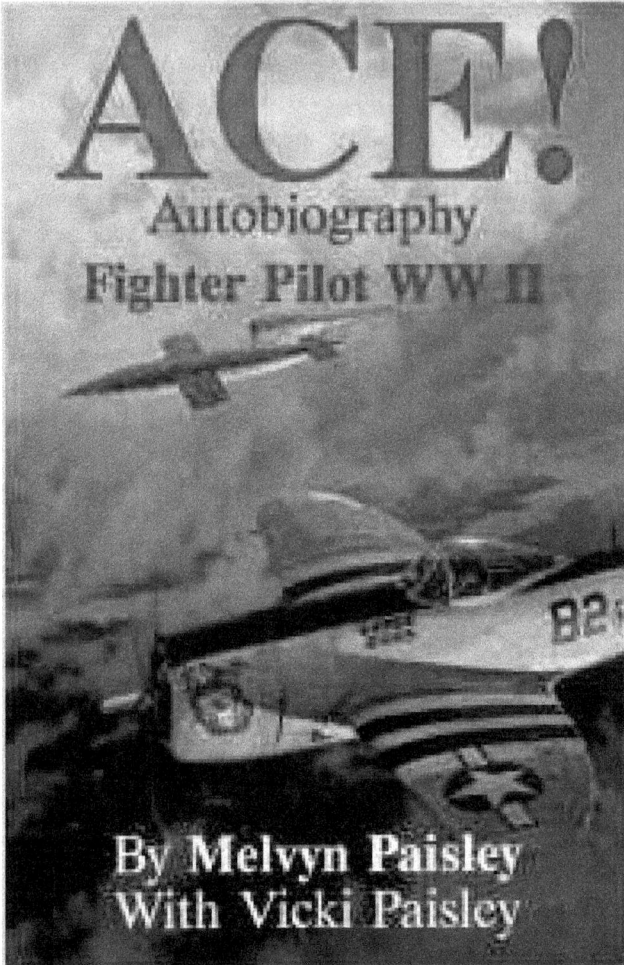

ACE!
Autobiography
Fighter Pilot WW II

By Melvyn Paisley
With Vicki Paisley

WAR

6. AN ACE AMONG CROOKS

Before Reagan's election, Paisley, as Director of International Sales for Boeing Aerospace in Seattle, managed Boeing's end of a four-year contract with Lehman's Abington Corporation. John Lehman was then selling his personal government expertise and high-level contacts earned during the Ford Administration for substantial retainers from TRW, Northrop and Boeing's military arm, Boeing Aerospace.[108] In those years, Lehman worked with Paisley to sell Chinook helicopters to the British Royal Air Force and nearly two-dozen Airborne Warning and Control System (AWACS) aircraft to NATO.[109] About the time Lehman thought he wouldn't be nominated as Reagan's Secretary of Navy, it was Bush, "a former naval aviator and friend of Lehman's, who had a private talk with Reagan and quietly convinced him that Lehman would be the best man for the job."[110] Lehman wrote that he answered his ringing telephone on January 22, 1981, and was asked, "Could you please hold the line for the President?" After a few seconds, Reagan said, "John, I'd like you to be the Secretary of the Navy. Welcome aboard."

Lehman received several false messages about being selected before the decision was completed, which might explain a discrepancy.[111] Lehman's published account seems at odds with the memory of Ron LeBailly, Vietnam-era combat helicopter pilot and son of retired Air Force three-star General Eugene Bernard "Ben" LeBailly, who had worked at Abington and then consulted for Boeing.[112] Captain LeBailly remembers being with his father, Lehman and Paisley in a waiting area at SeaTac Airport when Lehman got the word he would be Reagan's nominee for Secretary of the Navy:

> Lehman was disappointed, because he'd been hoping to be Secretary of Defense but he was too young or something.[113]

LeBailly also remembered:

> From that moment Paisley knew he would be working as Lehman's Assistant Secretary.[114]

Lehman liked Paisley for his hard-driving, ace fighter pilot attitude, and because he seemed to be able to get things done. LeBailly remembers his father thinking differently:

> Ben did not agree and believed Lehman should not be considering Paisley for a position with the government, because he was a crook.[115]

General LeBailly proved prescient, because Paisley

became the highest-ranking defense department civilian ever convicted in a pentagon procurement scandal. The U.S. Justice Department called its investigatory operation: ILL WIND. It's not clear why Lehman quietly left the office of Secretary of Navy just as Operation Ill Wind climaxed, but it's crystal clear that Lehman and Paisley were friends. Lehman greatly admired Paisley and expended much of his formidable bureaucratic talent getting him confirmed by the U.S. Senate.[116]

In early May 1981, Lehman visited Gerald Cann who held the position of Assistant Secretary for Research, Engineering and Systems and he told him he wanted Paisley in that position. Cann called Paisley and offered the position, remaining for the time being as Paisley's Principal Deputy. On July 8, the Counsel to the President, Fred Fielding, requested a special investigation of Paisley.[117] On July 16, Boeing's Security Office arranged for FBI interviews of nearly thirty people who knew Paisley. All interviews were favorable except that of James Gaines, which was completed under different circumstances. Gaines first asked if his answers could be kept confidential but continued to believe they would not be. He said he worked with Paisley in International Sales. He expressed reservations about Paisley's mental health and characterized him as a "good hater." Gaines refused to recommend Paisley for a government position, because, he said, "he will not be loyal to the United States." He then refused further comment.[118] On August 8, while Lehman was fishing in British Columbia with Paisley, Millie McGettrick wrote U.S. Senate Armed Services Committee Chairman John Tower and the *Washington Post* telling about bribery, a questionable bank account in Switzerland, poor emotional stability around women, continual lying and questions surrounding the death of his second wife. She wrote that Paisley had her fake a community property agreement in the name of the second wife after her death:

> I know what he is capable of doing, and I don't feel this is the person that should be making government decisions. I fear for my life and I will for at least five years. But you had to know, Melvyn Robert Paisley has no morals.[119]

Lehman responded publicly to her assertions by saying he looked into the allegations when he returned from fishing in British Columbia. He did so by asking the Navy's General Counsel:

Was there anything to indicate that Paisley wasn't fit for the job?

He said he was told the FBI had a collection of risqué allegations about Paisley's private life, but he admitted expecting that from his friend's colorful lifestyle. He inquired no further and didn't ask the Reagan Administration to reassess.[120]

On September 29, an FBI courier delivered the results of its Special Investigation to the White House, noting:

. . . no inquiries were made as to the sources of Paisley's income.[121]

The White House immediately gave Paisley his security clearance, and he began moving around the Pentagon where his bare-knuckle, prizefighter quality struck others as out of place.[122] On October 8, Paisley drew an $180,000 severance payment from Boeing and retired effective October 31. On October 23, the White House announced Reagan would nominate Paisley, indicating that in 1953 he had graduated from the American Institute of Technology rather than the American Television Institute of Technology, and MIT rather than dropping out of MIT in 1954.[123] On November 12, the Deputy Counsel for the Commandant of the Marine Corps helped Paisley write a letter and financial statement for Chairman Tower. The Marine attorney told subsequent investigators that Paisley did not inform him about his severance check, though he should have, given the briefings he'd received. On November 18, Paisley's confirmation hearing lasted nine minutes, with two of seventeen Senate Armed Services Committee members attending, including senior member "Scoop" Jackson. No one asked to see the FBI report and White House aides didn't show it. Jackson endorsed his constituent's military and industry accomplishments, calling Paisley a "fast mover." Several in the audience giggled. On November 23, 1981, the *Congressional Record* announced Paisley's confirmation. By

December, Paisley started reviewing $7 billion to $15 billion worth of contracts, growing to $40 billion annually. They included all Trident nuclear submarine and missile work recommended by the Chief of Naval Materials, before Paisley eliminated that office.[124] By then, Archbishop Hunthausen's effective opposition to the Trident program and his remarks to the Lutheran gathering in Tacoma were more than six months old.

To counter the threat, Paisley, always looking for a fighter pilot's edge, would have been in contact with a former employee from Anaconda, Montana, who had graduated from Montana State University's School of Engineering and was actively practicing Catholicism in Seattle. He was also brother to a very high level U.S. Army Joint Logistics General. Paisley would call his old employee Charles "Chuck" McLean.

NOTES

[108] Andy Pasztor, *When the Pentagon Was for Sale, Inside America's Biggest Defense Scandal*, Scribner, New York, NY, 1995, page 74.

[109] Pasztor, page 75.

[110] Vistica, page 85, base on interview of Pendleton James, March 30, 1994.

[111] Lehman, pp. 108-111.

[112] af.mil/information/bios/bio.asp?bioID=6155

[113] Author's telephone interview of Ron LeBailly, April 23, 2011.

[114] Ibid.

[115] Ibid.

[116] John B. Driscoll, "The Biggest Crook of Them All," *Steward Magazine*, Spring, 2012, stewardmagazine.com/Current_Issue/Spring_2012.html

[117] FBI FOIPA Request Number 1165672-000

[118] Ibid.

[119] Ibid; Also Author's interview of Millie McGettrick in Spokane, Washington.

[120] Pasztor, pp. 106-107.

[121] FBI Summary Memorandum for the Special Investigation of Paisley.

[122] Pasztor, pp. 85 & 107.

[123] presidency.ucsb.edu/ws/index.php?pid=4316#axzzlfl

[124] FBI interview of Gerald Cann.

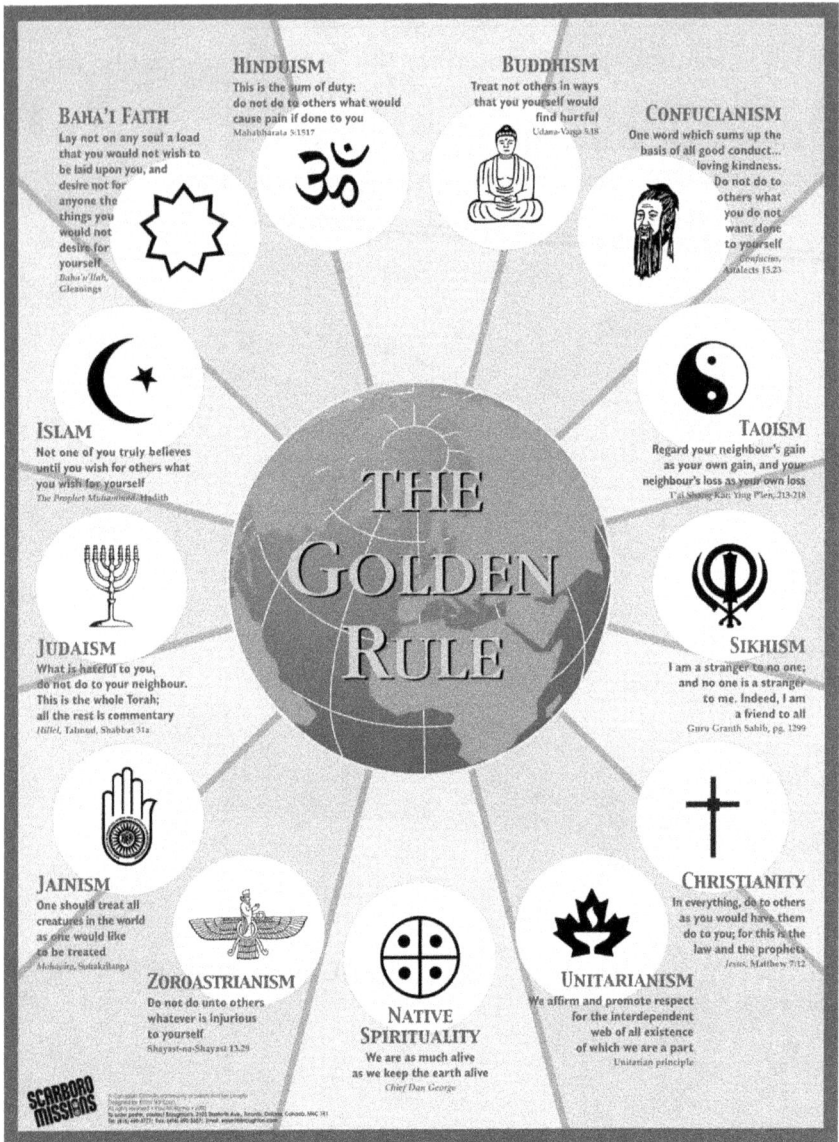

HUMAN DIGNITY

7. INDIVIDUAL CONSCIENCE

McLean once worked for Paisley on the Minuteman Missile Project in Boeing's Applied Physics Laboratory. That was before Paisley left for Montana as Boeing's respected on-site

Project Manager, helping to bring the first ten missiles, JFK's "Ace in the Hole," to operational readiness during the Cuban Missile Crisis.[125] In Seattle between 1959 and 1961, Paisley managed work on the missile's radio launch control system by the close-knit Electrical Engineers and Technicians, known as Paisley's "Black Gang." Without authorization, they frequently experimented with easily hidden miniature listening devices; more powerful bugging devices that could listen through walls and windows; and technology that could intercept and transmit telephone conversations long distances.[126] Paisley used these gadgets for what he called "counterespionage efforts." Others thought he used them to gather information on business competitors and rivals inside of Boeing.[127]

In the late 1960's, after Fluke Engineering of Everett, Washington, purchased a highly successful Montana State University spin-off company called Montronics, one of McLean's former professors recruited him to leave Boeing for Fluke.[128] There McLean worked as a "Minutemaner", highly respected for having worked on the Minuteman for Boeing.[129] That first $247 million Minuteman missile manufacture and assembly contract established a huge nuclear and a global aerospace presence. In 1983, McLean worked for Fluke and its co-locations with Boeing signaled an integrated business relationship. Fluke's symbiosis with Trident manufacturer, Lockheed, becomes even more obvious with a visit to the Fluke Corporate Headquarters Museum, which contains models of nuclear submarines from founder John R. Fluke's friend and fellow WWII naval officer, Admiral Hyman Rickover. There's a picture of Fluke looking over his shoulder at the camera while he served as Chairman of the 1970 Blue Ribbon Panel to Study Defense Department Procurement Policy, which justified building the Trident Weapon System. This was the year Nixon's National Security Advisor, Dr. Henry Kissinger, aided by a young assistant name John F. Lehman, threw his support behind the Underwater Launch Missile System. Secretary of Defense Melvin Laird gave Lockheed Corporation a cost plus deal, as the sole source for a new 6,000-mile range missile, and named the system Trident.[130] Chuck McLean's second son, Mark McLean, also an engineer, told me his dad worked for Lockheed in some kind of arrangement through Fluke on the Trident missile but kept the "Lockheed part of his life" apart from the family.[131] The older son, non-engineer Mike McLean, remembers his dad trying to tell him what he did. Though reluctant to talk about something that might be TOP SECRET thirty years earlier, the son said:

> All I can remember is that he was working on something called a 'synthesizer,' and he told me he wished he could be more of a hands on engineer as he'd been before, but after being away from doing the actual engineering for so long, he'd have to go back to school.[132]

On the Trident D5 missile re-entry body, there's at least one set of synthesizers developed by the Applied Physics Laboratory at Johns Hopkins University.[133] McLean kept close to his chest any classified work he was doing on this Trident Program technology.

McLean's friends at Knights of Columbus Council 6686 of Saint Brendan's Parish in Bothell, Washington, knew nothing about his professional life before the 1990's. That's when he started selling Knights of Columbus insurance. By then, according to his brother the General, McLean decided to stop being in charge of Fluke's manufacturing operations, because he felt the volume of defense work was driving down quality.[134] McLean was popular, respected and active in the Catholic Church around Seattle. After he died, the Washington State Knights of Columbus chartered a Charles F. McLean, Jr. Assembly 2621 in Kirkland.[135] Along with Grand Knight Mike Hanrahan, McLean started the Bothel Council, which I visited, eating dinner on bare folding tables before a scheduled night meeting. They were surprised but graciously yielded to my questions, recalling that McLean had sponsored his friend Hunthausen to be a Fourth Degree Knight in that very same room.[136] One remembered Hunthausen missing Vocation Night and sending a representative, because he had to go to a demonstration against nuclear weapons. All were adamant that regardless of the problems their archbishop might have for "letting homosexuals get close to the liturgy" or protesting nuclear weapons, no one in the Knights of Columbus would ever backdoor him with the Vatican. Hunthausen seemed loved and respected by all of them, especially Hanrahan, McLean's fishing buddy.

Hanrahan, an Irish immigrant who was a high school and college teacher over his lifetime, owned with his sons a commercial fishing boat. It was a gill-netter out of Everett named *Begorra*, which means "by God." From long hours on *Begorra* the two men became close friends. Hanrahan insisted:

> Chuck McLean was a good friend, a fine family man, a member of the Knights of Columbus, and a wonderful man. He should be up on a pedestal. I miss him deeply.

Hanrahan also considered Hunthausen to be a close friend, remembering him as a football coach, a priest, a bishop, an archbishop and the man who taught him how to tend bar. He insisted Hunthausen and McLean had a positive relationship, though at times they disagreed:[137]

> You've got to understand these were grown men. They're supposed to disagree and they told each other as much.[138]

Unlike McLean's two sons, Hanrahan did not realize McLean worked for Fluke well past November 1983. McLean's truck-designer son remembered his dad was "not happy about Hunthausen protesting against Trident nuclear weapons 'with his collar on.'" His father would say:

> It's as though Hunthausen's speaking for the Catholic Church, when he's just speaking for himself.

McLean's newspaperman son recalled his father's relationship with Hunthausen was "not all it should be at times." Revisiting with the General about his nephews' comments, he told me that at times "Charles" could be a little hot-headed. "Charles" confided in him once that, during Mass, he asked out loud for the rest of the congregation to pray for members of the clergy who wanted to withhold taxes that bought protective equipment for people like his brother who risked his life in Vietnam. He intimated that Hunthausen was furious, having just, at the same service, given a homily on the subject of withholding taxes. This still made the General laugh at his brother's antics. When I asked the General if his brother ever talked to him about Paisley, the General said, "No."[139]

If McLean did not tell his brother about Paisley, it seems he was just too busy living an active and engaged life to be part of an effort organized from Washington D.C. to dump his friend Hunthausen. Both sons remembered, "He was always busy with work and when he wasn't working, he was at the Knights of Columbus." He was already free to tell, and did tell, his disagreeable archbishop-friend what he felt was right, based on his own conscience. Having a truly pastoral Catholic bishop was a kind of outlet not always available to others. When Lutheran Pastor Martin Niemoller followed his conscience, he sat in the concentration camp at Dachau from fall 1937 until the end of the World War II.[140] As could happen anywhere, that individual conscience-smothering environment of Germany had become so extreme that by 1946 revered German national historian, Friedrich Meinecke, though he maintained some prejudices against Jews until his death in 1954, made a seminal realization. Regarding the cause of his nation's greatest misfortune and shame, he wrote:[141]

> The fundamental character of the Christian past rebelled against the Nazis . . . Liberalism and democracy, both things that Hitler ardently hated, also belonged, rightly understood, to this past and had been able to develop historically only on the basis of Christianity, through a graded series of modifications and secularizations. The right of freedom of conscience in predecessors to the American Constitution, such as the French Declaration of the Rights of Man and of the Citizen and, for example, the Rhode Island Constitution, had Christian roots. Hitler's totalitarianism

severed itself from recognition of the human conscience as capable of discerning above all the moral commandment to love one's neighbor as one's self. That single moral law implies human dignity in everyone else, and carries with it moral restraint, even in war between states.[142]

Had Meinecke lived 20 more years he would have certainly added the 1972 Montana Constitution to his list of improving protections for individual rights.[143] In addition to protecting a right to clean and healthful environment and open meetings, it contains a separate Declaration of Rights that include individual dignity and freedom of religion.[144] During the years of open gestation and application of this standard setting document, Bishop Hunthausen discussed its issues with his friends and neighbors. He voted for fellow Montanans to serve as Constitutional Convention Delegates or as State Legislators to implement it into law.

McLean's forthright disagreement with Hunthausen contrasts starkly with the fifth paragraph of Ratzinger's letter from the Congregation for the Doctrine of the Faith that closed the Apostolic Visitation to Seattle. The dogmatic theologian subsequently chosen to be Pope wrote:

> There is a need to correct misunderstandings concerning the role which conscience plays in making moral decisions. In particular it is necessary to highlight the valid claim on the Catholic conscience, which is made by the authoritative teaching of the church.[145]

The Catholic Church's Prefect for the Doctrine of the Faith at the time argued that individuals should defer to indifferent authority rather than thoughtfully, and with an open heart, sort out the essentials of a situation with the help of other human beings. Yielding to self-proclaimed authoritative teaching rather than working through the problem, requires a lazy indifference. Taking the time to really work through a question is a form of love. Elie Wiesel, an Auschwitz Concentration Camp survivor was right:

> The opposite of love is not hate, its indifference.[146]

McLean could tell his brother, the General, that something serious was going to happen to Hunthausen, either because he knew from Paisley calling to pump him for information or from Hunthausen himself confiding in McLean as a friend. One way or another, we can safely say that McLean wrestled with his own conscience as had Hunthausen, instead of remaining indifferent.

In a 2003 oral history, Peter Bridges, Deputy Chief of Mission in the U.S. Rome Embassy between 1981 and 1984, best summarized the fallout from the Apostolic Visitation:

> It was not because the situation required it. It was said at the time that the American Catholic hierarchy did not want to see American diplomatic relations with the Vatican, fearing that it would bring about a larger Vatican fist over the American Catholic Church, something which perhaps has eventuated since the establishment of full diplomatic relations.[147]

By 1990, when Laghi left the United States he had nominated 18 archbishops and 134 bishops, comprising 44 percent of U.S. Bishops. Some say he made the organization more conservative, which is an inappropriate political statement.[148] The conclusion that clearly applies is that he made America's prelates much more deferential to the Vatican and less pastoral to their flocks.[149] But this can change even under the weight of indifferent Vatican doctrine. The most dogmatic of people can change dramatically. In 2009, Rueda's family scattered his ashes into the Gulf Stream just after he counseled internet contenders in Miami's Mass Wars to extend an "open hand of unconditional friendship, regardless of ideology or morality." In his last message he wrote:

> . . . no institution, ritual, scripture or doctrine is at the core of religious praxis, but the human person . . .

He quoted Christ:

> . . . the Shabat (Sabbath) was made for man and not man

for the Shabat.[150]

NOTES

[125] Author's telephone interview of Major General Robert F. Goldsworthy, December 1, 2011.

[126] Pasztor, page 96.

[127] Ibid, page 97.

[128] Author's interview of Mike McLean in Spokane, Washington, November 11, 2010; Email exchanges with "the Gray Geeks," former Montana State University Electrical Engineering Faculty in the Bozeman, Montana, area, coordinated by Dr. Robert Maher, Professor and Department Head, Electrical and Computer Engineering, Montana State University, Bozeman, Montana, January 4, 2011.

[129] Pasztor, page 48.

[130] John F. Lehman, *Command of the Seas,* pp. 193-194.

[131] Authors telephone interview of Mark McLean in Renton, Washington, April 25, 2011.

[132] Author's interview of Mike McLean.

[133] Exchange of emails on April 25, 2011, with Michael H. Boehme, Global Engagement Department of Johns Hopkins University regarding his article, "Miniature Analog GPS Translators." jhuapl.edu/techdigest/TD/td2902/Boehme.pdf

[134] Authors interview of General William "Tim" McLean (Retired) in Butte, Montana.

[135] cee-nt.ce.wsu.edu/KofC/WSChistoryAddendum.pdf

[136] Author's visit with members of Bothel, Washington, Council 6686 prior to their regular meeting November 10, 2010.

[137] Author's telephone interview of Mike Hanrahan, May 19, 2011.

[138] Ibid.

[139] Author's interview of General McLean.

[140] http://en.wikipedia.org/wiki/Martin_Niemoller

[141] Ibid, pp. 85-86.

[142] Ibid, pp. 83-84.

[143] http://leg.mt.gov/bills/mca_toc/CONSTITUTION_II.htm

[144] http://leg.mt.gov/bills/mca_toc/CONSTITUTION_II_II.htm

[145] Ratzinger to Hunthausen, letter dated September 30, 1985, Paragraph 5.f.

[146] goodreads.com/athor/qotes/1049.Elie_Wiesel

[147] Bridges Oral History Interview.

[148] chron.com/CDA/archives/archive.mpl/1987_441066/vatican-s-u-s-envoy-defends-handling-of-hunthausen.html

[149] Thomas Reese, "The Laghi Legacy," *America,* June 23, 1990, http://www.americamagazine.org/conent/article.cfm?article_id=11379

[150] lexetlibertas.wordpress.com/2009/07/24/miami-mass-wars/

AFTERWORD

We baby-boomers are in the eighth stage of our human development. We're weighing the integrity of our lives against despair. For some, this balancing will bring wisdom, though many will never get wise even in the presence of many helpful thoughts we might consider.[151] In 1949, recently naturalized and ordained Father Louis, Thomas Merton, wrote:

> Ultimately, faith is the only key to the universe. The final meaning of human existence and the answers to the questions on which all our happiness depends cannot be found in any other way.[152]

In 1950, William Faulkner, in Stockholm accepting the Nobel Prize for Literature, said:

> Our tragedy today is a general and universal physical fear so long sustained by now that we can even bear it. There are no longer problems of the spirit. There is only the question: When will I be blown up? Because of this, the young man or woman writing today has forgotten the problems of the human heart in conflict with itself which alone can make good writing because only that is worth writing about, worth the agony and the sweat. He must learn them again. He must teach himself that the basest of all things is to be afraid; and, teaching himself that, forget it forever, leaving no room in his workshop for anything but the old verities and truths of the heart, the old universal truths lacking which any story is ephemeral and doomed---love and honor and pity and pride and compassion and sacrifice.[153]

In 1951, President Harry Truman touched on some of those verities. He had used nuclear weapons and, previously as a U.S. Senator, led the Investigative Committee that effectively corrected problems of waste, inefficiency and war profiteering during World War II. In Philadelphia, dedicating the Temple of the Four Chaplains, he observed:

Those four chaplains carried out the moral code, which we are all supposed to live by. They obeyed the divine commandment that men should love one another. They really lived up to the moral standard that declares: 'Greater love hath no man than this, that a man lay down his life for his friends.' They were not afraid of death because they knew that the word of God is stronger than death. Their belief, their faith, in His word enabled them to conquer death. This is an old faith in our country. It is shared by all our churches and all our denominations. These four men represented the Protestant, the Catholic, and the Jewish beliefs. Each of these beliefs teaches that obedience to God and love for one's fellow man are the greatest and strongest things in the world.[154]

NOTES

[151] Erik H. Erikson, Joan M. Erikson and Helen Q. Kivnick, *Vital Involvement in Old Age, The Experience of Old Age in Our Time*, W.W. Norton and Company, New York, NY

[152] Thomas Merton, *The Seeds of Contemplation*, New Directions Publishing, 1986,

[153] William Faulkner, Address Upon Receiving the Nobel Prize, December 10, 1950.

[154] President Harry Truman, Address at the Dedication of the Chapel of the Four Chaplains, February 3, 1951.

SEATTLE ARCHBISHOP RAYMOND G. HUNTHAUSEN

APPENDIX A:

Archbishop Raymond G. Hunthausen[155]
"Controlling Nuclear Arms with Non-Violence,"
Tacoma, Washington, June 12, 1981.

I am grateful for having been invited to speak to you on disarmament because it forces me to a kind of personal disarmament. This is a subject I have thought about and prayed over for many years. I can recall vividly hearing the news of the atomic bombing of Hiroshima in 1945. I was deeply shocked. I could not then put into words the shock I felt from the news that a city of hundreds of thousands of people had been devastated by a single bomb. Hiroshima challenged my faith as a Christian in a way I am only now beginning to understand. That awful event and its successor at Nagasaki sank into my soul, as they have in fact sunk into the souls of all of us, whether we recognize it or not.

I am sorry to say that I did not speak out against the evil of nuclear weapons until many years later. I was especially challenged on the issue by an article I read in 1976 by Jesuit Father Richard McSorley, titled "It's a Sin to Build a Nuclear Weapon." Father McSorley wrote:

"The taproot of violence in our society today is our intention to use nuclear weapons. Once we have agreed to that, all other evil is minor in comparison. Until we squarely face the question of our consent to use nuclear weapons, any hope of large-scale improvement of public morality is doomed to failure."

I agree. Our willingness to destroy life everywhere on this earth for the sake of our security as Americans is at the root of many other terrible events in our country.

I was also challenged to speak out against nuclear armament by the nearby construction of the Trident submarine base and by the first-strike nuclear doctrine which Trident represents. The nuclear warheads fired from one Trident submarine will be able to destroy as many as 408 separate areas, each with a bomb five times more powerful than the one used at Hiroshima. One Trident submarine has the destructive equivalent of 2,040 Hiroshima bombs. Trident and other new weapons systems such as the MX and cruise missiles have such extraordinary accuracy and explosive power that they can only be understood as a buildup to a first-strike capability. First-strike nuclear weapons are immoral and criminal. They benefit only arms corporations and the insane dreams of those who wish to "win" a nuclear holocaust.

I was also moved to speak out against Trident because it is being based here. We must take special responsibility for what is in our own back yard. And when crimes are being prepared in our own name, we must speak plainly. I say with deep consciousness of these words that Trident is the Auschwitz of Puget Sound.

Father McSorley's article and the local basing of the Trident are what awakened me to a new sense of the gospel call to peacemaking in the nuclear age. They brought back the shock of Hiroshima. Since that re-awakening five years ago, I have tried to respond in both a more prayerful and more vocal way than I did in 1945. I feel the need to respond by prayer because our present crisis goes far deeper than politics. I have heard many perceptive political analyses of the nuclear situation, but their common element is despair. It is no wonder. The nuclear arms race can sum up in a few final moments the violence of tens of thousands of years, raised to an almost infinite power - a demonic reversal of the Creator's power of giving life. But politics is itself powerless to overcome the demonic in its midst. It needs another dimension. I am convinced that a way out of this terrible crisis can be discovered by our deepening in faith and prayer so that we learn to rely not on missiles for our security but on the loving care of that One who gives and sustains life. We need to return to the Gospel with open hearts to learn once again what it is to have faith.

We are told there by our Lord: "Blessed are the peacemakers. They shall be called children of God." The Gospel calls us to be peacemakers, to practice a divine way of reconciliation. But the next beatitude in Matthew's sequence implies that peacemaking may also be blessed because the persecution which it provokes is the further way into the kingdom: "Blessed are those who are persecuted in the cause of right. Theirs is the kingdom of heaven."

To understand today the gospel call to peacemaking and its consequence, persecution, I want to refer especially to these words of our Lord in Mark:

"If anyone wants to be a follower of mine, let that person renounce self and take up the cross and follow me. For anyone who wants to save one's own life will lose it; but anyone who loses one's life for my sake, and for the sake of the Gospel, will save it" (Mk. 8:34-35).

Scripture scholars tell us that these words lie at the very heart of Mark's Gospel, in his watershed passage on the meaning of faith in Christ. The point of Jesus' teaching here is inescapable: As his followers, we cannot avoid the cross given to each one of us. I am sorry to have to remind myself and each one of you that by "the cross" Jesus was referring to the means by which the Roman Empire executed those whom it considered revolutionaries. Jesus' first call in the Gospel is to love of God and one's neighbor. But when he gives flesh to that commandment by the more specific call to the cross, I am afraid that like most of you I prefer to think in abstract terms, not in the specific context in which our Lord lived and died. Jesus' call to the cross was a call to love God and one's neighbor in so direct a way that the authorities in power could only regard it as subversive and revolutionary. "Taking up the cross," "losing one's life," meant being willing to die at the hands of political authorities for the truth of the Gospel, for that love of God in which we are all one.

As followers of Christ, we need to take up our cross in the nuclear age. I believe that one obvious meaning of the cross is unilateral disarmament. Jesus' acceptance of the cross rather than the sword raised in his defense is the Gospel's statement of unilateral disarmament. We are called to follow. Our security as people of faith lies not in demonic weapons which threaten all life on earth. Our security is in a loving, caring God. We must dismantle our weapons of terror and place our reliance on God.

I am told by some that unilateral disarmament in the face of atheistic communism is insane. I find myself observing that nuclear armament by anyone is itself atheistic and anything but sane. I am also told that the choice of unilateral disarmament is a political impossibility in this country. If so, perhaps the reason is that we have forgotten what it would be like to act out of faith. But I speak here of that choice not as a political platform - it might not win elections - but as a moral imperative for followers of Christ. A choice has been put before us: Anyone who wants to save one's own life by nuclear arms will lose it; but anyone who loses one's life by giving up those arms for Jesus' sake, and for the sake of the Gospel of love, will save it.

To ask one's country to relinquish its security in arms is to encourage risk - a more reasonable risk than constant nuclear escalation, but a risk nevertheless. I am struck by how much more terrified we Americans often are by talk of disarmament than by the march to nuclear war. We whose nuclear arms terrify millions around the globe are terrified by the thought of being without them. The thought of our nation without such power feels naked. Propaganda and a particular way of life have clothed us to death. To relinquish our hold on global destruction feels like risking everything, and it is risking everything - but in a direction opposite to the way in which we now risk everything. Nuclear arms protect privilege and exploitation. Giving them up would mean our having to give up economic power over other peoples. Peace and justice go together. On the path we now follow, our economic policies toward other countries require nuclear weapons. Giving up the weapons would mean giving up more than our means of global terror. It would mean giving up the reason for such terror - our privileged place in the world.

How can such a process of taking up the cross of non-violence happen in a country where our government seems paralyzed by arms corporations? In a country where many of the citizens, perhaps most of the citizens, are numbed into passivity by the very magnitude and complexity of the issue while being horrified by the prospect of nuclear holocaust? Clearly some action is demanded - some form of non-violent resistance. Some people may choose to write to their elected representatives at the national and state level, others may choose to take part in marches, demonstrations or similar forms of protest. Obviously there are many ways that action can be taken.

I would like to share a vision of still another action that could be taken: simply this - a sizable number of people in the state of Washington, 5,000, 10,000, 500,000 people, refusing to pay 50 percent of their taxes in nonviolent resistance to nuclear murder and suicide. I think that would be a definite step toward disarmament. Our paralyzed political process needs that catalyst of non-violent action based on faith. We have to refuse to give incense - in our day, tax dollars - to our nuclear idol. On April 15 we can vote for unilateral disarmament with our lives. Form 1040 is the place where the Pentagon enters all of our lives and asks our unthinking cooperation with the idol of nuclear destruction. I think the teaching of Jesus tells us to render to a nuclear-armed Caesar what that Caesar deserves - tax resistance. And to begin to render to God alone that complete trust, which we now give through our tax dollars to a demonic form of power. Some would call what I am urging "civil disobedience." I prefer to see it as obedience to God.

I must say in all honesty that my vision of a sizable number of tax resisters is not yet one, which I have tried to realize in the most obvious way - by becoming one of the number. I have never refused to pay war taxes. And I recognize that there will never be such a number unless there are first a few to give the example. But I share the vision with you as a part of my own struggle to realize the implications of the Gospel of peace given us by our Lord. It is not the way of the cross which is in question in the nuclear age, but our willingness to follow it.

I fully realize that many will disagree with my position on unilateral disarmament and tax resistance. I also realize that one can argue endlessly about specific tactics, but no matter how we differ on specific tactics, one thing at least is certain. We must demand over and over again that our political leaders make peace and disarmament, and not war and increased armaments, their first priority. We must demand that time and effort and money be placed first of all toward efforts to let everyone know that the United States is not primarily interested in being the strongest military nation on earth, but in being the strongest peace advocate. We must challenge every politician who talks endlessly about building up our arms and never about efforts for peace. We must ask our people to question their government when it concentrates its efforts on shipping arms to countries which need food, when it accords the military an open checkbook while claiming that the assistance to the poor must be slashed in the name of balancing the budget, when it devotes most of its time and energy and money to developing war strategy and not peace strategy.

Creativity is always in short supply. This means that it must be used for the most valuable purposes. Yet it seems evident that most of our creative efforts are not going into peace but into war. We have too many people who begin with the premise that little can be done to arrange for a decrease in arms spending since the Soviet Union is bent on bankrupting itself on armaments no matter what we do. We have too few people who are willing to explore every possible path to decreasing armaments.

In our Catholic Archdiocese of Seattle I have recommended to our people that we all turn more intently to the Lord this year in response to the escalation of nuclear arms, and that we do so especially by fasting and prayer on Monday of each week. That is the way, I believe, to depend on a power far greater than the hydrogen bomb. I believe that only by turning our lives around in the most fundamental ways, submitting ourselves to the infinite love of God, will we be given the vision and strength to take up the cross of nonviolence.

The nuclear arms race can be stopped. Nuclear weapons can be abolished. That I believe with all my heart and faith, my sisters and brothers. The key to that nuclear-free world is the cross at the center of the Gospel and our response to it. The terrible responsibility which you and I have in this nuclear age is that we profess a faith whose God has transformed death into life in the person of Jesus Christ. We must make that faith real. Life itself depends on it.

Our faith sees the transformation of death through the cross of suffering love as an ongoing process. That process is our way into hope of a new world. Jesus made it clear that the cross and empty tomb didn't end with him. Thank God they didn't. We are living in a time when new miracles are needed, when a history threatened by overwhelming death needs resurrection by Almighty God. God alone is our salvation, through the acceptance in each of our lives of a non-violent cross of suffering love. Let us call on the Holy Spirit to move us all into that non-violent action which will take us to our own cross and to the new earth beyond.

NOTES

[155] Alan J. Stein, *History-Link Profile Essay*, June 09, 2013

PRESIDENTS RONALD REAGAN AND PETER GRACE

APPENDIX B:

PRESIDENT REAGAN'S LAST SPEECH
CATHOLIC KNIGHTS OF MALTA DINNER
WALDORF ASTORIA HOTEL, NEW YORK CITY
JANUARY 13, 1989.[156]

Your Eminences (Cardinals O'Connor, Hickey, and Law), Your Excellency (Archbishop Laghi), Your Most Eminent Highness (Grand Master Berte), President Peter Grace, ladies and gentlemen. Tonight for me is a moment for humility. To stand here, before you, the members of the most ancient order of its kind in the world, formed in the Holy Land 900 years ago -- or as some of us would say, only yesterday. But to stand in this way before the members of this order with its remarkable history -- which speaks to the entire ebb and flow of Western Civilization-- and its noble present, which is a monument to the highest values of free men and women, is to be reminded once again that the only true calling of man is service to God, and to have served in that calling is cause not for pride but for gratitude.

Today, as for nine centuries, you, the Knights and Dames of Malta, serve the victims of poverty, hunger, and disease. I have often noted that in America we have a tradition that began when the first community of settlers joined together to help build a home for a newcomer -- the tradition of neighbor helping neighbor, the tradition of the barn raising and the settlement house and the church-run hospital. The tradition that Tocqueville spoke of in wonderment more than a century-and-a-half ago when he observed that when there was a job to do, Americans didn't wait for the Government, but pitched in and did it themselves.

Yes, an American tradition, but one more ancient and universal, as well, of which history offers few examples more crystalline and enduring than the Knights of Malta.

Now, if I may tell you a story. You don't find this spirit of love and mercy everywhere -- which makes you appreciate it all the more when you do find it. When I was still fairly new in my former line of work, the movie business, I was cast to play opposite Errol Flynn in a picture called *The Santa Fe Trail*. The movie was really about John Brown, the abolitionist who led the famous raid on Harper's Ferry. Raymond Massey played John Brown, and he gave his character that perfect touch of insanity. Mike Curtiz directed and I've always thought the studio picked the perfect man to direct a film about a madman. To give you an idea of what I mean, we had reached the end of the picture, the scene in which they hang John Brown, when Mike flew into one of his rages. He was furious. He'd just discovered he couldn't actually hang Massey; he'd have to use a dummy instead. Then he started moving around the actor who was playing the minister who stood by Brown on the scaffolding. He was setting up the shot, looking through the camera viewfinder, and motioning to the actor to move about -- first left, then right, finally back. The poor fellow took one step too far back, fell 12 feet from the scaffolding, and broke his leg. Mike walked across, looked down where he lay on the ground, turned to his assistant, and said, "Get me another minister." If only I could treat Congress that way.

But to return to faith, hope and love. Your work with the ill – in particular, those with leprosy, now those with AIDS; your partnership with AmeriCares and its president, Bob Macauley, to move medicine to those in need all over the world; your support of Mother Theresa's care for the poorest of the poor; your work feeding the hungry in Latin America: These are some of the highest examples of love, compassion, and mercy in our time. They show the power of faith moving in the modern world.

I've heard a lot about this being the era of greed - usually from those who really mean that taxes are too low and government is too small. I wish these critics would explain how it is that in the past 8 years, during this supposed era of greed, charitable giving has risen to record highs in our Nation. And not too long ago we found it's even higher than we thought. No one – it turned out – had ever fully added up what Americans give to their neighbors in need through their churches, synagogues, and other religious organizations. Some of this was because of the difficulty of gathering the information. But I expect that it may also have reflected a secularist bias. Whenever we've talked about the immensity of American giving, critics have been quick to retort that much of it is through church congregations and that not much of that goes to the poor and the hungry. Now a private organization, called Independent Sector has added up what America's congregations actually do pass on – not just conjectured about it – it found that the giving to the needy from those sources amounts to more than half of the national total. In other words, we already knew that private giving in America through corporations, foundations, and other easily seen bodies was the highest in the world – and now we know that this giving is only about a third of all American private givings to the needy. That sure doesn't sound like greed to me.

By the way, I suspect that a dollar that comes from our churches and synagogues goes farther to help those in need than one that comes from the Government – and I don't mean just because the Government's overhead is higher. No, it's that the State's power is, at its root, the power to coerce, for example, to demand taxes. The power of the Church is the power of love. And that makes all the difference.

Why is it that, in this city which spends so much on its social service bureaucracy, so many young people find their refuge and salvation in Father Ritter's Covenant House? Could it be that there, in the priests and nuns and volunteers they see the face of love entering their lives for the first time? They aren't a case to be handled, which they would be if they were in the hands of the Government agencies, but a soul to be cherished.

Twenty years ago the Government declared a war on poverty. Poverty won. Too many poor people were sucked into a system that declared that the only sin is not to have enough money. Soon, too many became dependent on government payments and lost the moral strength that has always given the poor the determination to climb America's ladder of opportunity. In my view, the great lesson of that experience is that no war on poverty stands a chance unless it rises above the secular state and is guided by the power of love that moves through God's word.

Now, I know that when the Knights talk of the power of love and of serving "the least of these they brethren," you also mean – as I do – protecting the unborn. Our critics call themselves pro-choice but have they ever stopped to think that the unborn never have a choice?

When Roe v. Wade goes – as I have faith it must – the way of

Dred Scott and "separate but equal," a new debate will rise in the State Houses of our land. And the voice that I believe must be heard and, in the end, shall be heard over all the others is the voice of life. The knights can be part of that voice. Can I count on you?

In just 7 days I will lay down the mantle of this great office the American people have bestowed upon me. I won't leave the battle. As long as there is breath in me, I will fight for the principles in which I believe. But if I may, in this moment of leaving office make two special requests of you. The first is that you prepare now to be part of that voice of life in the great debate ahead. And the second, that you help America find a way out of the trap of the welfare state. Help it find a way to open the doors of hope and love, open them as no state, any state, ever can, for those in need. Help open the promises of this land of shining opportunity to all.

I believe now, as I always have, that America's strength is in "We the People." This great experiment in faith and freedom will rise or fall on the courage of "We the People." And you who have so willingly and ably taken up the burdens of freedom, through the Knights and throughout your lives, you who are surely part of what Jefferson called our "natural aristocracy" you will surely be in the front as "We the People" turn to the dawn of America's tomorrows.

Thank you and God bless you.

NOTES

[156] White House Files, document 60642755 in File SP 1316, Reagan Presidential Archives, Simi Valley, California

LEHMAN AND REAGAN FIRING ADMIRAL RICKOVER.[157]

APPENDEX C:

SECRETARY OF NAVY JOHN F. LEHMAN'S SPEECH:
"THE IMMORALITY OF UNILATERAL DISARMAMENT,"
IN THE TEMPLE OF THE FOUR CHAPLAINS
PHILADELPHIA, SUNDAY, MARCH 7, 1982

Today we do more than honor the memory of the great sacrifice made by these men of God, the heroic four chaplains. We also honor their spirit of patriotism, a spirit that sees no contradiction between serving God and serving in the defense of our nation in time of peace or war. They knew that the great traditions of the faiths they represented have always viewed as honorable the defense of human values and freedoms - as the three altars bear silent but vigilant witness. This great spirit can be summed up by the traditional American phrase "For God and country." It is a phrase that has always been closely tied to duty and honor.

I believe that this spirit has been shared by the vast majority of men and women who - down through history to the current day - have dedicated their lives to God and to their fellow men through religious vocation. We can be thankful that in their time they did not support the kind of pacifist ideology that has - most unfortunately - now captured a small and idealistic, but vocal minority within the religious community. That wiser majority never called upon their countrymen to lay down their arms in the face of the totalitarian advance. Today, I am sorry to say, that call is being issued by a few of our countrymen.

They did not urge others in the clergy and the souls in their care to stop building those weapons that alone stand between freedom and slavery for our nation and its allies - weapons whose sole purpose is to defend our values and way of life. Such urging is now taking place.

Today we are told by a few religious spokesmen that even possession of nuclear arms by the United States is a grave evil. But all the evil seen in their lifetimes would pale beside the evil that our unilateral disarmament would inevitably produce in this country and throughout the world.

We are told that our effort to arm other nations so they might better resist communist aggression is somehow immoral. I ask, where is the morality in Poland- in Afghanistan - in Ethiopia, Cambodia, Vietnam - in Hungary, Czechoslovakia and inside the Soviet Union? Can we expect morality - or justice - or restraint - from a godless ideology? No, we cannot History has proven that. What we can expect is oppression, power and precious little mercy.

Those voices calling for unpreparedness and naked trust refer to themselves, naively I believe, as "the church of peace." What they are calling for would produce not only war - but the eventual loss of all freedoms for all mankind - religious freedom included.

Peace is not the result of unilateral disarmament. It never has been. And it never will be. Peace doesn't just happen; it must be forged. Peace must be made. That is why the Bible speaks of "peacemakers." Blessed are the peacemakers. This refers not merely to those who speak the words of peace, but also - and with equal appropriateness - to those who take action to preserve peace. Even those of us who strongly agree that our Judeo-Christian tradition not only allows but, at times, demands, the ability and willingness to use force to protect our most precious human values, have not been energetic enough. We have taken too much for granted. We have stood by silently while vocal advocates of unilateral disarmament on the part of the United States have sought to capture public attention -and been lionized by the media.

In a particularly tasteless example of this unfortunate trend, the Catholic bishop of Seattle publicly called our new naval submarine base at Bangor, Washington, "an American Auschwitz." Such an ignorant and repugnant statement illustrates how far the abuse of clerical power has been taken by a few religious leaders. There is, I believe, something deeply immoral in the use - or misuse - of sacred religious office to promulgate extremist political views.

I fully recognize that pacifism is an aspect of the religious tradition we honor today: But it is only one aspect of that tradition, and historically it has never held the prevailing view in determining moral questions of war and peace.

In responding to criticisms on the naming of the nuclear submarine Corpus Christi, I expressed my concern with the theme that naval ships and even military service were considered somehow profane. I pointed out that commanders and crews of our naval vessels recognize fully that their essential mission is to keep the peace - and that it is vitally important that all Americans remember the humanistic values of peacekeeping.

What is needed today, more than ever, is a firm reaffirmation of the great religious tradition that has always subtended our willingness to defend our Judeo-Christian Western values. We must realize - and remind our fellow countrymen - that this fashionable pacifism we see and hear today - as well intended as it may be -cannot and will not lead to peace. To disarm before a totalitarian aggressor does not lead to peace. More often, as history teaches, it leads to war. In the past it led to death camps and persecution -to a very real Auschwitz and the Gulag - to the Katyn Forest and the Vietnamese boat people.

Whenever and wherever the voices that would unilaterally disarm us are heard, I am concerned as a Catholic and as a citizen that they have not understood the clear words of the pope and his secretary of state on this important subject.

This country must remain armed to ensure peace. In this bitterly contested, turbulent world, we are both focus and rallying point for those who would be free - and for the highest expressions of individual, political and religious thought.

America is the chief hope of Western Judeo-Christian civilization. For this reason we must have the courage to speak out and reaffirm the great religious traditions that support our determined efforts. Should we not speak out, we may wake up one morning and find we have lost a war of propaganda waged against a strong American defense, a war of ideas put forward by a zealous, uninformed and unrepresentative minority in the name of valid religious values invalidly applied.

The learned Justice Louis Brandeis once said, "The greatest dangers to liberty lurk in insidious encroachment by men of zeal and well-meaning, but without understanding." It is our responsibility - that of each American - to speak out and to see this danger contained. We must demonstrate that our -deepest and most profound religious beliefs and values allow us to say - no.they demand that we say - that we are determined to arm our nation so that freedom will not be crushed.

When I became secretary of the navy I took a solemn vow to protect and defend the Constitution of the United States. My oath was given before my fellow countrymen - and it was given before God. I do not take that oath lightly. And I disagree vehemently with those who would suggest that religious values should force me to follow policies of unilateral disarmament which would make mockery of that vow. I see no conflict between my duty and my religious beliefs. To the contrary - my religious beliefs provide vital inspiration to my efforts.

Today, tomorrow and on into America's future, let us join together in reaffirming those religious traditions that alone give our defense efforts meaning and value - and a sense of higher purpose. Let us take pains to remind a new generation that "God and country" is a religious as well as patriotic phrase and that the defense of freedom is a positive and proper act in the eyes of the Almighty.

We are now embarked in Washington on a new budget cycle for 1983. As always, our democratic process will ensure a lengthy and complex debate. The result will undoubtedly be the balanced expenditure of scarce national resources to provide equitable services to all Americans. If specious argument by a few uninformed and overly idealistic religious leaders bias this process to the disfavor of national defense, the result could be grave. The current balance of power in the world is not that favorable to the interests of our nation - and the trends, given Soviet growth and adventure, are ominous. In this decade America may well be seeing its last chance to become strong again and deter future incursions against us. I am pledged to see that we do not let this chance pass.

We Americans are proud of our freedom, of our history and of our efforts to further self-determination throughout the world Throughout America's two centuries our idealism - when properly focused - has consistently provided benefit to mankind: Within this decade America will reverse past trends that have weakened her -and will again be sufficiently strong to influence world events for the profoundly humane causes of freedom and justice.

America should also be proud of the great health and vitality of religion - of all religions - in our land. One of the keys to our national success is to remain the God-fearing and God-trusting people we have always been. "In God we trust" is not a hollow national slogan. It is, fittingly, the acknowledgment that Americans have always been profoundly aware of the ultimate origin of all their national blessings - and of the considerable kindnesses we enjoy in geography, history, resources and the character of our people. Let it always be so.

NOTES

[157] George C. Wilson, "Rickover Is Forced To Retire," *The Washington Post*, November 14, 1981.

TEMPLE OF THE FOUR CHAPLAINS

APPENDIX D:

PRESIDENT HARRY TRUMAN'S ADDRESS[158]
DEDICATING THE CHAPEL OF THE FOUR CHAPLAINS
PHILADELPHIA, FEBRUARY 3, 1951

Dr. Poling, associate chaplains, and ladies and gentlemen:

This chapel commemorates something more than an act of bravery or courage. It commemorates a great act of faith in God.

The four chaplains whose memory this shrine was built to commemorate were not required to give their lives as they did. They gave their lives without being asked. When their ship was sinking, they handed out all the life preservers that were available and then took off their own and gave them away in order that four other men might be saved.

Those four chaplains actually carried out the moral code which we are all supposed to live by. They obeyed the divine commandment that men should love one another. They really lived up to the moral standard that declares: "Greater love hath no man than this, that a man lay down his life for his friends."

They were not afraid of death because they knew that the word of God is stronger than death. Their belief, their faith, in His word enabled them to conquer death.

This is an old faith in our country. It is shared by all our churches and all our denominations. These four men represented the Protestant, the Catholic, and the Jewish beliefs. Each of these beliefs teaches that obedience to God and love for one's fellow man are the greatest and strongest things in the world.

We must never forget that this country was founded by men who came to these shores to worship God as they pleased. Catholics, Jews, and Protestants, all came here for this great purpose.

They did not come here to do as they pleased--but to worship God as they pleased, and that is a most important distinction.

The unity of our country comes from this fact. The unity of our country is a unity under God. It is a unity in freedom, for the service of God is perfect freedom.

If we remember our faith in God, if we live by it as our forefathers did, we need have no fear for the future.

Today, many people have become full of fear. If we reaffirm our common faith we can overcome these fears.

This does not mean that we can always be sure what the future will bring. We cannot always know what the outcome of events will be. President Lincoln once said, "The Almighty has His own purposes."

But we need not be afraid of the outcome if we go on trying to do the right thing as God gives us to see the right.

That is what we are trying to do in the world today. We are trying to establish world peace, so that all men can live together in brotherhood and in freedom. And to do that, we are working with other nations to create the rule of law in the world.

And what does this rule of law mean? Let me give you an example. In the early days of our western frontier, law and order were not yet established. Disputes were settled in favor of the man who was quickest on the draw. Outlaws terrorized whole communities.

Men who wanted to see law and order prevail had to combine against the outlaws. They had to arm themselves. At times they had to fight. And after they had put down lawless violence, the courts took over and justice was established. And then it was possible for all citizens to get on with the important work of building up their own communities, paving the streets and building schools, and giving all the people a chance at the right kind of life.

That is just what we are trying to do today in the international field. If we can put a stop to international aggression, order can be established and the people of the world can go ahead full speed with the constructive tasks of peace.

We are not trying to do this job by ourselves. We could not do it by ourselves if we tried. We are acting as one member of a whole community of nations dedicated to the concept of the rule of law in the world. As in all other communities, the members of this community of nations have many different ideas and interests and do not all speak with one voice. Some are cautious and some are impatient.

We cannot always have our own way in this community. But we have a tremendous responsibility to lead and not to hang back.

Fate has made this country a leader in the world. We shirked our responsibility in the 1920's. We cannot shirk it now. We must assume that responsibility now, and it will take everything we have--all the brains and all the resources that we can mobilize.

Leadership carries with it heavy responsibilities. Good leaders do not threaten to quit if things go wrong. They expect cooperation, of course, and they expect everyone to do his share, but they do not stop to measure sacrifices with a teaspoon while the fight is on.

We cannot lead the forces of freedom from behind.

The job we face is a hard one. Perhaps it will be harder in the few years immediately ahead than it will be in the years thereafter. If we can get over the present crisis successfully--if we can restrain aggression before it bursts into another world war, then things will be easier in the future. And I think we can do this. We can't be sure, of course, but there is good reason to hope for success.

In recent months the United Nations has been faced with a serious challenge. But it is meeting that challenge courageously, and it is still man's best hope of establishing the rule of law in the world.

General Eisenhower has brought home the report that the people of Europe, in spite of their difficulties and their many problems, want to preserve their freedom. He has told us of the effort they are making. They are working very hard, and if we all work together, we can be successful.

When things look difficult, there are always a lot of people who want to quit. We had people like that in the Revolutionary War, and we have had them in every war and every crisis of our history. Thomas Paine called them summer soldiers and sunshine patriots. If we had listened to them, we would never have been a free and independent nation. We would never have had a strong and prosperous country. We would not be strong enough now to stand up against Communist aggression and tyranny.

The sacrifices that are being made today by the men and women of this country are not being made in vain. Our men are in Korea because we are trying to prevent a worldwide war. The men who have died in Korea have died to save us from the terrible slaughter and destruction which another world war would surely bring.

Their sacrifices are being made in the spirit of the four chaplains in whose memory this chapel is dedicated. They are being made in defense of the great religious faiths, which make this chapel a place of worship. These sacrifices are being made for the greatest things in this life, and for the things beyond this life.

I have faith that the great principles for which our men are fighting will prevail.

NOTES

[158] The President spoke at 3:10 p.m. at the chapel in the Russell H. Conwell Memorial Church, Broad and Berks Streets, Philadelphia, Pa. In his opening words he referred to Dr. Daniel A. Poling, chaplain of the sanctuary and father of one of the four World War II heroes. The chapel was dedicated on the eighth anniversary of the torpedoing of the American troop-ship Dorchester off the coast of Greenland. The four chaplains were Lt. John P. Washington, Catholic, Lt. Alexander D. Goode, Jewish, and Lts. George L. Fox and Clark V. Poling, Protestant.

ASSISTANT SECRETARY OF THE NAVY FOR RESEARCH,
ENGINEERING AND SYSTEMS, MELVYN R. PAISLEY

APPENDIX E:

SPECIAL FBI REPORT TO THE WHITE HOUSE CONCERNING
MELVYN R. PAISLEY

September 29, 1981
BY COURIER

Honorable Fred F. Fielding
Counsel to the President
The White House
Washington, D.C.

Dear Mr. Fielding:

In accordance with a request received from you on July 8, 1981, an investigation has been conducted concerning Mr. Melvin Robert Paisley. Transmitted herewith is a summary memorandum containing the results of this investigation.

Sincerely yours,
Charles P. Monroe
Assistant Director
Criminal Investigation Division
Enclosure
CEC: mb (VI) (4)

Note: Investigation of Mr. Paisley, Director of International Sales for the Boeing Aerospace Company, Seattle, Washington, who is being considered for Presidential appointment as an assistant secretary of the Navy, complete. Allegations of bribe taking, involvement in the death of his second wife wire tapping of a fellow Boeing employee and extra marital affairs with future wives set forth. Three individuals who requested confidentiality, declined to recommend.

RETURN TO (XXRedactedXX) ROOM 5158

September 29, 1981
MELVIN ROBERT PAISLEY

THE INVESTIGATION OF MR. PAISLEY COVERED INQUIRIES AS TO HIS CHARACTER, LOYALTY, AND GENERAL STANDING, BUT NO INQUIRIES WERE MADE AS TO THE SOURCES OF HIS INCOME.

Birth

Mr. Paisley was born on October 9, 1924, in Portland, Oregon.

Education

Mr. Paisley attended U.S. Grant High School, Portland, Oregon, until February 1943. He was issued his high school diploma on June 13, 1952.

Mr. Paisley indicated that he attended the Northwest School of Commerce, Portland, Oregon, from October 1945, to October 1946, receiving no degree. This attendance could not be verified due to unavailability of records.

He indicated that he attended the American Institute of Technology, Chicago, Illinois, from 1951 to 1953. Upon interview, Mr. Paisley furnished a diploma from the American Television Institute of Technology (ATIT), Chicago Illinois indicating that he received a Bachelor of Science in Television Engineering degree on September 25, 1953. No records independent of his diploma are available to confirm his attendance at this institution inasmuch as ATIT has been out of existence for many years.

Mr. Paisley attended Massachusetts Institute of Technology, Cambridge, Massachusetts, from September

1953, to February 1954, receiving no degree.

Military Service

A review of Mr. Paisley's military file at the Regional Office of the Veterans Administration, Seattle, Washington disclosed that he entered the United States Army Air Corps on February 8, 1943, and served on active duty until April 14, 1944, when he was discharged as an enlisted man. On April 15, 1944, he reentered on active duty in cadet training as a pilot and remained on active duty until November 10, 1945, when he was honorably discharged as a captain.

CEC: mb (VI)

-1-

Melvin Robert Paisley

Employment

Mr. Paisley has indicated that from October 1946, to September 1951, he was self-employed at the Roseway Lunch, Portland, Oregon. This could not be verified due to unavailability of records and the fact that buildings in the locale of the former Roseway Lunch have long been demolished in connection with an urban redevelopment project.

Since March 1954, Mr. Paisley has been employed by the Boeing Aerospace Company, Seattle, Washington, where he is presently Director of International Sales.

Mr. Paisley was also a partner in the consulting firm of Holman Paisley, Seattle, Washington, from 1956 until 1962, when the firm dissolved.

Family Status

Mr. Paisley is married to the former (-Redacted-) and they reside at (-Redacted-), Washington.

Mr. Paisley has indicated his wife is a United States citizen.

Records of the Superior Court of the State of Washington for King County, Seattle, Washington, disclose that Mr. Paisley and his first wife, (-Redacted-) were divorced on April 17, 1962, on the grounds of unhappy differences in the marital life. Mr. Paisley was the defendant in this action.

Records of the Seattle-King County Department of Public Health, Seattle, Washington, disclose that Mr. Paisley's second wife, Mary Lou Paisley, died on May 8, 1968, in Kent, Washington. An autopsy was performed and her death was ruled accidental. Cause of death was listed as acute pulmonary adema (sic.) as a possible consequence of drug hypersensitivity brought on by ingestion of two doriden tablets.

Records of the Superior Court of the State of Washington for King County, Seattle, Washington, disclose that Mr. Paisley was divorced from his third wife, (-Redacted-) on March 29, 1980, on the grounds of incompatibility. Mr. Paisley was also the
defendant in this action.

-2-

Melvin Robert Paisley

Mr. Paisley's father, Frank Paisley, is deceased.

In addition to his wife, Mr. Paisley has listed the following living close relatives:

Mother Clara Maria Paisley
Portland, Oregon

Brother(-Redacted-)
Portland, Oregon

Son(-Redacted-)
Seattle, Washington

Son(-Redacted-)
Seattle, Washington

Based on the background information provided by
Mr. Paisley, he has no close relatives residing in
communist-controlled countries.

Interviews

1. An individual, who requested and was granted
confidentiality and who knew Mr. Paisley during the
period he was married to (-Redacted-) from 1951 until
1962, provided the following information:

This individual characterized Mr. Paisley as a liar
and of poor moral character and stated that his marriage
to (-Redacted-) failed because of his involvement with
other women. This individual opined that Mr. Paisley was
very loyal to the United States, and was a very capable,
hardworking man with leadership qualities, but declined to
recommend him for a position with the Government
because he is "not an honest person."

2. A second individual, who requested and was granted
confidentiality and who knew Mr. Paisley during the
period he was married to his third wife, (-Redacted-) from

January 1969, to March 1980, provided the following information:

Mr. Paisley had been dating (-Redacted-) for approximately two years while still married to Mary Lou Cole Paisley, his second wife. Mr. Paisley told this individual that he would "get rid" of his second wife to avoid being "taken" in a divorce settlement as he believed to have been the case with his first wife, and had requested (Redacted) to forge Mary Lou Cole Paisley's name to a community property

1. (-Redacted-) Seattle, Washington, Mr. Paisley's (-Redacted-)2. (-Redacted-) Spokane, Washington, Mr. Paisley's (-Redacted-)

-3-

Melvin Robert Paisley

agreement that he filed after her death. Mr. Paisley also advised this individual that he had "wiretapped" the office of fellow Boeing employee named (-Redacted-) concerning a job promotion matter but provided no additional details regarding that incident, and could provide nothing to substantiate this allegation.

This individual additionally alleged that Mr. Paisley took a sewing machine and a trip to Hawaii as a bribe from the Singer Company concerning a contract, and that while still married to McGetrick (sic.) he had an affair with his present wife, (-Redacted-), for two years. This individual declined to recommend Mr. Paisley for a position with the Federal Government.

3. A third individual, who requested and was granted confidentiality, provided the following information:

This individual opined that Mr. Paisley was in good physical health but expressed reservations about his mental health and characterized him as a "good hater." Opining that Mr. Paisley would not be loyal to the United States, this individual refused to recommend Mr. Paisley for a position with the United States Government but would not elaborate on this opinion.

4. A fourth individual, who requested and was granted confidentiality, provided the following information:

This individual, who has known Mr. Paisley for eight years, stated that he/she considers Mr. Paisley to be a person of integrity and good moral character who deals fairly and honestly with others. This individual characterized Mr. Paisley as a leader who enjoys an excellent reputation in the community and who is unquestionably loyal to the United States. This individual highly recommended Mr. Paisley for a position of trust and responsibility with the United States Government and commented that he would perform brilliantly in any Government position.

(-Redacted-), Seattle, Washington, stated that he has known Mr. Paisley for approximately four years and considers him to be in excellent physical and mental health. He characterized Mr. Paisley as an open-minded leader who exercises good judgment and is friendly and outgoing. He highly recommended Mr. Paisley for a position of trust and responsibility in any government position.

3. James E. Gaines, Research and development department Boeing Aerospace Company, Seattle Washington.

4. Michael Coleman, Marketing Manager, Boeing Aerospace Company, Seattle, Washington.

Melvin Robert Paisley

Mr. John Palowez, Seattle, Washington, a retired Boeing Aerospace Company employee and former neighbor of Mr. Paisley's, described him as shrewd and intelligent. He noted that though Mr. Paisley may have had some personality conflicts with his work associates he has always been diplomatic and professional in his dealings with others. Mr. Palowez stated that he has no reason to question Mr. Paisley's loyalty, and recommended him for a position of trust and responsibility with the Federal Government.

Mr. Oliver C. Boileau, President, General Dynamics Corporation, Clayton, Missouri advised that he has been acquainted with Mr. Paisley for the past twenty years. He was President and Mr. Paisley was Vice President of International Affairs at Boeing Company, Seattle, Washington. He characterized Mr. Paisley as intelligent and flamboyant, and as a person of outstanding executive ability and integrity. He highly recommended Mr. Paisley for a position of trust with the United States Government.

Thirty-five additional persons, consisting of current and former supervisors and colleagues, present and former neighbors, references, professional associates, and social acquaintances, were interviewed. They advised Mr. Paisley is a loyal American whose character, reputation, and associates are above reproach. He was described as hardworking, aggressive, innovative, intelligent, competent, and dedicated. They recommended him for a position of trust and responsibility.

Among those additionally interviewed are the following:

Claus G. Claesson, Assistant to the Director of Contracts for International Projects, Boeing Aerospace Company, Seattle, Washington.

Howard N. Stuverude, Vice President and General Manager of Missile Systems, Boeing Aerospace Company, Seattle, Washington.

Ben T. Plymale, Vice President, Advanced Missile Programs, Boeing Aerospace Company, Seattle, Washington.

John Crosetto, Program Manager, Short Range Air Defense Program, Boeing Aerospace Company, Seattle, Washington.

John E. Schmick, Director of Product Extension, Boeing Aerospace Company, Seattle, Washington.

Robert L. Brock Vice President for Space Systems, Boeing Aerospace Company, Kent, Washington.

-5-

Melvin Robert Paisley

H.E. Hebeler, President, Aerospace Division, Boeing Aerospace Company, Kent, Washington.

Robert Edwin Davis President and Chairman of the Board of Directors, Thiokol Corporation, Newton, Pennsylvania.

John Joseph Brett, Vice President, Singer-Kearfott Corporation Little Falls, New Jersey.

Credit and Arrest Checks

Information has been received from appropriate
credit reporting agencies indicating their files contain
either no record or no additional pertinent information
concerning Mr. Paisley.

Information has been received from appropriate
law enforcement agencies indicating their files contain no
record concerning Mr. Paisley or his close relatives, except
the following:

Records of the King County Department of Public Safety
Seattle, Washington, disclose that Mr. Paisley was arrested
on April 2, 1965, on a charge of nonsupport based on the
complaint of his former wife, (-Redaced-). Bail was set at
$3000.00; however, the case was stricken from the court
calendar before trial based on a resumption of
support payments by Mr. Paisley.

These records also disclose that Mr. Paisley's son, (-
Redacted-) was arrested for forgery on February 24, 1977.
No record of a disposition of this charge could be located.

Security Clearances

Mr. Paisley holds two active top secret clearances
granted to him on February 12, 1965, and April 4, 1979, by
the Defense Industrial Security Clearance Office, the
employing agencies being the Boeing Company, Seattle,
Washington, and ITT World Communications,
Incorporated, New York, New York, respectively.

-6-

Melvin Robert Paisley

Miscellaneous

Records of the Security Office, Boeing Aerospace Company, Seattle, Washington contain no additional pertinent information regarding Mr. Paisley.

Records of the King County Superior Court, Seattle, Washington, contain a document titled, "Agreement as to Status of Community Property After Death of One of the Spouses," entered into by Mr. Paisley and his second wife, Mary Lou Paisley, on December 15, 1965, and notarized that same date. This document was filed for record by the county auditor on July 2, 1968, at the request of "M.R. Paisley."

Agency Checks

Information has been received from the following governmental agencies indicating their files contain either no record or no additional pertinent information concerning Mr. Paisley:

Division of Personnel Investigations; Office of Personnel Management; Central Intelligence Agency; Defense Central Index of Investigations; Defense Industrial Security Clearance Office; Security Division, Office of the Secretary of Defense; United States Army Investigative Records Repository; United States Secret Service; and the White House Office.

The central files of the FBI, including the files of the Identification Division, contain no additional pertinent information concerning Mr. Paisley.
DECLASSIFIED DATE: 1-7-87[159]

The cause was cancer, said his wife, Vicki.

Mr. Paisley was a central target in what prosecutors said was the most sweeping and successful operation against white-collar fraud in the multibillion-dollar industry that sells equipment to the Defense Department.

By the time Mr. Paisley was sentenced, the investigation had resulted in the convictions of 9 government officials, 42 Washington consultants and corporate heads and 7 military contractors.

Mr. Paisley's case provided an extensive look into the "revolving door" world of military contractors in a period of intensified military spending under President Ronald Reagan.

In 1991, Mr. Paisley admitted accepting hundreds of thousands of dollars in bribes from Navy contractors whom he helped while he was the senior Navy official responsible for research, engineering and systems. In court documents, he acknowledged his role in three major plots, although he was also implicated in others.

The cases included helping an Israeli manufacturer of pilotless reconnaissance planes win several contracts in return for cash sent to a Swiss bank account and providing confidential information to the Sperry Corporation to win a bid for the Aegis weapons system.

He was sentenced to four years in prison and fined $50,000 after a judge rejected his request for home detention on the grounds that he was suffering from prostate cancer.

It was a grim end to a career that began with promise.

Mr. Paisley was born on Oct. 9, 1924, in Portland, Ore. He spent his early years in a logging camp, where his father was a logger and his mother was a cook. He enlisted in the Army Air Corps in World War II, where he became a skilled pilot and downed several enemy planes over Europe. He received the Distinguished Service Cross and the Silver Star. After the war, Mr. Paisley studied engineering and was hired by the Boeing

Corporation. In 28 years there, he rose to become international sales manager.

He established a close relationship with John F. Lehman Jr., who asked him to move to Washington after Mr. Lehman was named Navy secretary. They established a reputation for brash, occasionally heavy-handed management and for slashing red tape that interfered with the Navy's expansion. Mr. Lehman was never accused of any misdeeds. Before he headed to the Pentagon, Mr. Paisley received a $183,000 severance package from Boeing. Prosecutors sued him under the federal ethics law in 1986, arguing that such a large "golden handshake" would compromise Mr. Paisley's objectivity toward Boeing. The Supreme Court later ruled that such packages were not, in themselves, illegal.

In his Pentagon post, which he left in 1987, and later as a consultant to the arms industry, Mr. Paisley used his influence and inside information to guide executives from businesses like Martin Marietta and United Technologies through the procurement thicket, steering billions of dollars in contracts their way.

Released from prison in 1995, he spent his time painting and collecting World War II films. He was a consultant for a two-hour documentary, "Shooting War," narrated by Tom Hanks and recently broadcast on ABC-TV, Ms. Paisley said.

Also surviving are four children from previous marriages, Deborah, of Sumner, Wash., Frank, of Golden, Colo., Melvyn Jr., of Los Angeles, and Beaumante, of Seattle; a sister, Dorothy; and two grandchildren.

NOTES

[159] FBI Freedom of Information/Privacy Act Request : 1165672-00.
[160] Christopher Marquis, "Obituary for Melvyn R. Paisley, a former top Navy official and a fighter ace who was involved in a military procurement scandal in the 1980's that involved bribery, bid rigging and insider advice, died on Dec. 19. He was 77 and lived in McLean, VA;" New York Times , December 21, 2001.

APOSTOLIC DELEGATE ARCHBISHOP JEAN JADOT

APPENDIX F:

ARCHBISHOP JEAN JADOT OBITUARY
CLERIC WHO SHAPED U.S. PASTORAL CHURCH DEAD AT 99
John A. Dick[161]
National Catholic Reporter
Brussels, Belgium, January 21, 2009

Archbishop Jean Jadot died peacefully at his residence in Brussels Jan. 21. He was 99. He had been apostolic delegate to the United States from 1973 to 1980, and at the direction of Pope Paul VI, he transformed the U.S. episcopal leadership by appointing pastorally oriented bishops.

With family and friends near him, Jadot had received Communion and last rites a couple of days before his death. Archbishop Karl-Josef Rauber, the apostolic nuncio to Belgium, had come to his bedside with a special papal blessing from Pope Benedict XVI.

Jadot's first episcopal appointee was Bernard Law in December 1973 and his last one was Kenneth Untener in November 1980. In his seven years as apostolic delegate, he was responsible for the appointments of 103 new bishops and the assignments of 15 archbishops: William Borders to Baltimore; Patrick Flores to San Antonio; Peter Gerety to Newark, N.J; James Hickey to Washington; Raymond Hunthausen to Seattle; Francis Hurley to Anchorage, Alaska; Oscar Lipscomb to Mobile, Alabama; Edward McCarthy to Miami; John May to St. Louis; Edward O'Meara to Indianapolis; John Quinn to San Francisco; John Roach to Saint Paul, Minn; Charles Salatka to Oklahoma City; Robert Sanchez to Santa Fe, N.M; and Rembert Weakland to Milwaukee.

Jadot became the hero of progressive post-Vatican II Catholics in the United States. The bishops appointed upon his recommendation were quickly known as (and denounced by conservative American Catholics as) the "Jadot boys." After the 1976 Call to Action gathering in Detroit, and especially after an address to the American bishops in Washington on Nov. 9, 1976, in which Jadot told the bishops what their agenda should be for the sake of the church in the United States, the apostolic delegate became the target of bitter animosity from conservative bishops and laypeople. A close friend in Rome warned him at that time that "they" would now be "out to get him."

In "A Watchman for the House of Israel," his 1976 address to the general meeting of the National Conference of

Catholic Bishops in Washington, Jadot gave a candid assessment of the state of the Catholic church in the United States, stressing three areas of concern. He began with the shortage of priests:

> This morning, my brother bishops, I would like to share with you some of the signs that I read in our times so that we can see from afar and be prepared for what is coming. One problem that we will have to face very soon — at most within 10 years — is the shortage of priests. I ask your permission to be frank and candid. I am worried that so many of us — laity, clergy, and bishops — do not seem to be concerned that, if not today, then in a very few years, we will not be able to staff our parishes and institutions with priests as we did in the past. ... In some regions priests are dying in their 50s from overwork. Others are chronically tired and frustrated because they cannot accomplish by themselves what several priests together accomplished in the past.

He then went on to stress the need for "new forms of parochial life and perhaps new forms of parochial organization so that the parish can become a community of small communities." Then he called attention to the problems of minorities in the American church:

> How are we to give pastoral care to those who do not feel at home with our white, Western European ways of public worship and community living, to those who have not adapted and do not want to adapt to what we call our American way of doing things? ... How are we to foster the unity of the people of God within the one, holy, catholic, and apostolic church while at the same time preserving the diversity that is one of the riches of this great country?

A few bishops reacted with obvious irritation when he chided them about failures to promote social justice and respect for all cultures:

> I wonder if the majority of our priests and people realize our

shortcomings in these areas and even our arrogance toward our brothers and sisters in the faith who are in some ways different from ourselves. I wonder if we can ever fully understand the legitimate frustrations that they feel.

In his concluding remarks, the apostolic delegate called brief attention to two more areas of concern that the bishops would have to follow up on:

There are other problems either near or far on the horizon. I could mention the question of the role of women in society and in the church or problems that will come from the rejection of the traditional standards of morality in society, political and business life.

The apostolic delegate concluded his address to "my brother bishops" by saying:

Let us be confident, courageous and open to the Spirit. Let us build the church of God by our foresight.

A few American bishops were delighted with Jadot's observations. A number were dumbfounded. Some were outright angry. Clearly, after that November meeting in Washington, two divergent Jadot camps emerged in the United States.

New York Times religion writer Kenneth Briggs echoed the sentiments of more progressive American Catholics when he sketched the positive impact of the apostolic delegate in a Feb. 27, 1977 article titled "Pope's U.S. Delegate Takes Powerful Role." The anti-Jadot sentiments of conservative American Catholics were reflected in A.J. Matt's article on March 17 in *The Wanderer*: "Does Archbishop Jadot Echo Rome's Voice?" A few days later, on March 25, 1977, *National Catholic Reporter* editor Arthur Jones came out with a major Jadot interview titled "Jean Jadot: Pope's man in the U.S." That same issue of *NCR* included a very laudatory editorial titled "Jadot Urbi et Orbi."

The *NCR* editorial was the straw that broke the conservative American Catholic camel's back. From that time on, Jadot received a steady flow of anonymous hate mail (originating from Missouri) telling him to "get out of the United States and go back to Belgium." He was also being denounced at the Vatican. At one point Jadot even offered his resignation to Paul VI, who responded immediately by saying. "No. You are doing just what I want you to do."

Sentiments at the Vatican, however, would change significantly with the election of Pope Paul's second successor. In 1980, a physically worn-out Jadot offered his resignation to Pope John Paul II. It was happily accepted. Jadot was called to Rome, where he worked in obvious papal disfavor for four years, as pro-president of the Vatican Secretariat for Non-Christians.

Since 1984, he had been in active retirement in Brussels. Unlike his predecessors and his successor as apostolic delegate, Jadot was never named cardinal.

I vividly remember being with him the day the announcement came out about his successor, Archbishop Pio Laghi, being named cardinal. Jadot had called me that morning and asked if he could drive over to Louvain for lunch with his friends at The American College. At the time I had not yet heard the news, but learned what had happened while he was on his way from Brussels. We met and had a delightful lunch. No one said anything about Laghi. After lunch, I walked him back to his car. Just before he opened the door, he turned to me: "Did you hear the news?" "Yes," I said, "just after your phone call this morning." "Well," Jadot said, "I had to be with my American friends today. It is not important to be a cardinal. What bothers me is that I know this is not about being a cardinal. It is a slap in my face."

Jadot was born Nov. 23, 1909, in Brussels. He came from a well-known aristocratic Belgian family of engineers, bankers and railroad builders whose business dealings stretched throughout Belgium, as well as into China and the Belgian Congo. Two months before his 17th birthday, Jadot entered the Catholic University of Louvain. He was a bright but not always physically strong student. By 1930 he had already completed his doctorate in philosophy, graduating magna cum laude. His thesis was titled

"On the Thought of Alfred Edward Taylor." Jadot often said, with a wry chuckle:

> Fortunately they never published my doctorate. I would be so embarrassed today. I began my university studies much too young and lacked the necessary maturity. They gave me my degree more for my efforts than for any philosophical value of my work.

The same year that he completed his doctoral work at Louvain, Jadot entered the major seminary in Malines. He was happy about the direction of his life, but his father was not. Already in 1927, the older Jadot had sent his son to the United States on a get-acquainted-with-the-bigger-world-type business trip. His father hoped that Jadot would get a taste for the secular life and stop thinking about priesthood. Jadot returned with a fascination with Americans and their almost childlike innocence and spontaneity. And he still wanted to become a priest. A year later, his father sent him to Africa, again hoping to shift the direction of his son's life. Jadot returned with valuable insights into colonial Africa — a colonial Africa shaped in part by his own family. No more trips for a while.

On Feb. 11, 1934, Cardinal Josef-Ernest Van Roey in Malines ordained Jadot a priest. In the years immediately following his ordination, from 1934-1940, he was an associate pastor in suburban Brussels, and from 1939-1952 held various chaplaincies for youth as well as the Belgian military. From 1952 to 1960 he was chaplain to the Congolese troops in the then-Belgian Congo. From 1960 to 1968 he was Belgian national director of the Propagation of the Faith. During this time he was already attracting the attention of Pope Paul VI, thanks to the influence of Cardinal Joseph Suenens, who had taken a special interest in Jadot and recommended him to the attention of the Vatican Secretary of State.

In May 1967, when Archbishop Pietro Sigismondi, secretary of what is now called the Congregation for the Evangelization of Peoples, died very unexpectedly, Cardinal Josef

Frings from Cologne, Germany, recommended Jadot as his successor. In August, however, Pope Paul VI selected his friend Archbishop Sergio Pignedoli for the position. At the request of Pope Paul, one of Pignedoli's first responsibilities shortly after taking office in Rome was to prepare for the elevation of Jadot to the episcopacy so that "he will be able to represent the Holy See in a missionary country."

In early December 1967, as Jadot was preparing for his father's death (the older Jadot died on December 17), Cardinal Suenens got a phone call from Rome: Would he support the nomination of Jadot to the post of apostolic pro-nuncio to Thailand? Suenens immediately responded with an enthusiastic "Yes." Nothing officially was said to Jadot. In early January 1968, however, Jadot had picked up some gossip from a close friend who simply told him, "I have heard from XYZ that you are going to be appointed apostolic delegate to Bangkok … but you like me know nothing about this."

On Feb. 12, 1968, Archbishop Silvio Oddi, papal nuncio in Brussels, called Jadot. Oddi urgently had to speak with him about "the language problems at the University of Louvain." (Strong demands were coming from the Flemish-speaking Belgians that the university be separated into two autonomous universities, one French-speaking and one Dutch-speaking; and apparently the nuncio thought Jadot could supply him with some helpful background information about the situation.) Archbishop Oddi asked Jadot to meet with him. When he and Jadot met, they exchanged a few remarks about Louvain, but then the nuncio remarked:

> Actually I need to talk to you about something else. I have been charged to inform you that the Holy Father has elevated you to the episcopacy and appointed you apostolic pro-nuncio to Thailand. The telegram arrived this morning and I am to report back tomorrow morning that you have accepted. You have no reason to refuse. Reflect and pray. I expect to hear from you at 9:00 a.m. tomorrow.

Jadot's formal diplomatic ministry for the Holy See had begun. On May 1, 1968, Jadot was ordained bishop at the church of Our Lady of Grace outside Brussels by Cardinal Suenens; Archbishop Oddi; and André Marie Charue, Bishop of Namur, Belgium. From 1968 to 1971 he was apostolic pro-nuncio to Thailand and apostolic delegate to Laos, Malaysia and Singapore. From May 1971 to 1973 he was apostolic pro-nuncio to Cameroon and Gabon and apostolic delegate to Equatorial Guinea.

In April 1972, Jadot's mother was near death, and he returned to Belgium to be with her. (She died on April 22). Jadot was in poor health, literally worn-out from his travels and work in Africa. His doctors put him in a hospital in Lausanne for a few weeks of rest and also told him he had to get out of the tropical climate. Word, of course, got back to Rome.

On the anniversary of his episcopal ordination, May 1, 1973, Jadot, now back in Cameroon, returned to his residence around noon and found a letter on his desk marked "personal." He didn't think much of it, because by that time he was used to secret and personal communications about various issues. He opened the envelope and immediately found a second envelope hand-addressed by Vatican Secretary of State Cardinal Jean Villot. It was dated April 27. Villot informed him that Pope Paul VI had been looking for a new apostolic delegate for the United States and was thinking of him. Would he be willing to accept?

Jadot reflected and prayed. During the liturgy of May 2, the feast of St. Athanasius, Jadot was struck by a phrase taken from the Gospel according to St. John:

It is not you who have chosen me but I have chosen you ...
you will go and produce fruit and your fruit will be lasting.

On May 4, he wrote Cardinal Villot. Yes, he would accept — especially because the United States was not a tropical country!

In early July 1973, Jadot was in Rome to receive specific instructions about his new appointment. Pope Paul VI informed him that he had had been selected to "the most important of our posts" because he was not under the influence of the curia and would not have to follow in the footsteps of his two predecessors. Paul VI was very much aware of the fact that previous apostolic delegates had been pawns in the hands of powerful kingmaker American cardinals. Nor did Paul like the fact that most American bishops were, in his opinion, more big businessmen than they were pastors. It was time for a change. Archbishop Giovanni Benelli, from the Secretariat of State, had also informed the pope that several U.S. archbishops were pushing for a new kind of apostolic delegate, as well. Previous delegates Archbishop Egidio Vagnozzi and Archbishop Luigi Raimondi had in fact not been that well received.

Jadot was told he did not have to be the "eyes and ears of the pope," but he did have to "express his heart" to the church in the United States. Paul VI, Benelli and other key advisors from the Secretariat of State then outlined major characteristics of Catholics in the United States as well as their concerns. American Catholics were "faithful" and "generous," especially toward Third-World peoples; they had made great strides in Catholic education, thanks especially to the great numbers of religious; but there were also a number of red flags about the church in North America.

The pope was alarmed about a growing pro-abortion movement in the United Sates, a decline in the quality of religious instruction in Catholic schools, increased numbers of divorced people, and certain questionable theological positions being taught at American Catholic universities. Jadot was reminded about a comment made by Belgian Catholic theologian Edward Schillebeeckx shortly after he had returned from a tour of the United States:

> Rome should be paying more attention to the audacity developing within the United States than to what is happening in Holland.

Benelli stressed that there was a growing communication problem among American Catholics — between conservatives and progressives and between bishops and priests

— and added that the Holy See had lost much credibility in the United States. The new apostolic delegate would have to be a healer and a bridge-builder, someone who could establish "bonds of affection." Pope Paul told Jadot that he had selected him because he was not in the mold of previous delegates Vagnozzi and Raimondi. He expected Jadot to be a new kind of representative of the Holy See. Jadot understood what he meant and immediately sent a clear and highly symbolic message to the American hierarchy. He announced that he would not enter the United States by way of New York.

Jadot had been informed that previous apostolic delegates had arrived first of all in New York, where they were welcomed by the local archbishop, who thereafter considered the apostolic delegates his special friends. Cardinal Terence James Cooke, archbishop of New York, as soon as he had heard about Jadot's appointment, had written to Jadot that he was looking forward to welcoming Jadot to the United States and would be at the airport in New York to greet him. Jadot's reaction to Cooke was typically Jadot:

> I wrote Cardinal Cooke to thank him for his kind intentions but told him that since there was a direct flight to Philadelphia, which then went on to Washington, I would take this flight. It would be faster and I would not have to change planes. And that is what I did on July 12, 1973, accompanied by Msgr. Powers." (Msgr. Raymond T. Powers was secretary to the Apostolic Delegation Washington 1971-1977.)

Cooke was angry, considered Jadot's actions a personal affront, and never forgot this highly significant event. Jadot landed first in Philadelphia, where he went through customs, then flew on to Washington, where he was warmly greeted by, in his own words, "an impressive group of cardinals and bishops." Eight days after U.S. Independence Day celebrations in the nation's capital, the ninth apostolic delegate and the first non-Italian was immediately introduced to the high-speed pace of the American way of life.

Jadot arrived at the delegation in Washington at 5:30 p.m. and was given a few minutes to freshen up before a reception and banquet in his honor. "After 10 hours in an airplane," he commented, "it is not easy to improvise a response to a toast of welcome from a kind but teasing cardinal." Jadot, in the first hours of his assignment, made a hit with the hierarchy and finally got to bed at 10:30 p.m. — 20 hours without sleep after his departure from Rome. And he was at work early the next morning.

In Bangkok, Jadot had been assisted by one aide from the Vatican and an administrative secretary. In Washington, he discovered that he had a large administrative staff and six priest aides, four Americans and two Italians, from the Vatican. At 8:00 a.m. on July 13, when the mail arrived, Jadot astonished his new staff. It was the first of many changes that would surprise them. Jadot invited his secretaries to sit around the table with him as they went through the mail. Some weeks later, he was informed that his predecessors had never done such a thing. In the past the mail had been sorted by a seated senior aide while the secretaries stood in silence at the other side of the table.

The anti-Jadot campaign, I can reveal today, was spearheaded by Cardinals John Carberry of St. Louis, John Krol of Philadelphia and John Cody of Chicago. Carberry and Krol clearly had the ear of John Paul II and eventually convinced him that Jadot was "destroying the Catholic church in the United States." Cody was opposed to Jadot because he knew personally that Jadot had asked Paul VI to remove him.

One of my favorite tape-recorded Jadot recollections, in fact, is his account of his meeting with Paul VI about Cody. "I knew something had to be done about Cody," Jadot said, "so I went to Pope Paul VI. I stood before his desk. The Holy Father asked what I wanted. I said, 'Holy Father, I have come to ask for the head of John Cardinal Cody on a silver platter.' " Jadot thought Paul would acquiesce and was surprised at his reaction. "You don't understand. You don't understand," the pope replied, "I cannot do this because he is my friend." It seems that Cody and Paul VI had become friends, were in periodic telephone contact, and Pope Paul VI, clearly aware of the situation, still could not remove him. And so Cody stayed until his death in 1982. And under John Paul II, Jadot left in 1980, was kept out of the limelight at the Vatican for four years, and then retired.

I believe that American Catholic church history will be kind to Archbishop Jadot and that the words of the eminent American Catholic church historian John Tracy Ellis will someday be carved somewhere in stone:

> It was my good fortune to become a friend of this admirable churchman, and the more I studied him the more did I admire his dedication to the church, his high intelligence, his broad reading habits and his friendly approach.

NOTES

[161] John A. Dick, Jadot friend and biographer, now retired from the Catholic University of Louvain in Belgium.

INDEX

www.ingramcontent.com/pod-product-compliance
Lightning Source LLC
Chambersburg PA
CBHW060938040426
42445CB00011B/922